THE FIVE KEYS TO DISTANCE

HOW TO DRIVE THE GOLF BALL FARTHER

THE FIVE KEYS TO DISTANCE

HOW TO DRIVE THE GOLF BALL FARTHER

by

ERIC M. JONES

PGA CLASS "A" PROFESSIONAL
M.A. - SPORT PSYCHOLOGY

Limitation Of Liability

Golf by its very nature contains some inherent risk of injury. The information presented in this book is for your reference and entertainment, and you, as the reader/end-user, are ultimately responsible for judging the suitability of the exercises and activities as they relate to your unique circumstances. Please use good judgment. This book is not intended as legal or physical advice. If you are in doubt, consult a physician. While attempts have been made to verify information provided in this publication, neither the a uthor nor the publisher assumes any responsibility for errors, omissions, or contradictory information contained herein. No representations or warranties are made or implied, including with respect to the accuracy or completeness of the contents of the book or any claims for performance. Neither the author nor the publisher shall assume any liability for any damages, including special, incidental, consequential, or other damages whatsoever on behalf of the purchaser or reader of these materials.

Published by: Birdie Press
21 Orinda Way, Suite 236
Orinda, CA 94563

www.TargetCenteredGolf.com

ISBN: 978-0-9844-1710-0

This book is dedicated to the memory of Ernie Barbour—Friend, mentor, teacher. His guidance made all the difference, and as the consummate PGA Professional he set an example to which I continually aspire.

CONTENTS

	Preface	*ix*
	Acknowledgements	*xiii*
	Forward	*xv*
	Introduction	*xvii*
1.	It's All About Speed	1
2.	Developing Expertise In Speed	3
3.	The Elements Of Distance	7
4.	Understanding The Role Of Self-Awareness In Learning	15
5.	Distance Key #1: Balance	21
6.	Distance Key #2: Leverage	53
7.	Distance Key #3: Arc Width	71
8.	Distance Key #4: Speed of Hips	85
9.	Distance Key #5: Target Extension	101
10.	B.L.A.S.T Summary With Drills	115
11.	How To Practice	117
12.	Notes On The Swing	121
13.	How To Create A Reliable Pre-Shot Routine	127
14.	Taking It To The Course	137
	Index	*143*

Preface

Welcome To "The 5 Keys To Distance"

You can drive the ball farther than you do now, and this book is dedicated to helping you understand how..

My name is Eric Jones, PGA Professional and World Long Drive Champion. I am also the founder of the Seaver Golf Academy, home of an innovative approach to learning golf—The Golf Coach Program— and Target Centered Golf. *The 5 Keys to Distance* will help you drive it farther. Target Centered Golf is dedicated to helping you play your best golf. I invite you to visit the site at www.targetcenteredgolf.com.

I wrote *The 5 Keys to Distance* to help you understand the elements of DISTANCE: Where it comes from and how you can get more of it - using the swing you have today.

This book is **not** about fixing your swing. It's about helping you understand what you need to do to hit the ball farther.

The Focus Of This Book

You don't need a "perfect" golf swing in order to have distance. The primary focus of this book is how you can develop an "effective" golf swing for speed and therefore significantly more distance with the driver. And you'll more than likely find yourself adding distance to all your other clubs as well.

That means teaching you how to make the maximum use of your athletic ability with whatever swing you have right now to increase your clubhead speed through the impact zone. The goal is to get you 20 yards or more farther off the tee, and still find the fairway. Many of my students have achieved far more than 20 yards.

In this book I will help you gain an understanding of the three key factors that influence distance: clubhead speed, center contact, and angle of approach. As you read on, you'll discover that CLUBHEAD SPEED is the most important element necessary to gain distance. In order to maximize your speed (and correct center of contact and angle of approach), you'll need to follow the 5 Keys outlined in this book.

The Best Way To Use This Book:

This book outlines a specific, step-by-step program for you to follow to help build your fastest driver swing speed and to maximize your athletic abilities. Each key step of the program has multiple drills designed specifically for that component of the progression to help you understand what you should be doing in order to build skills and speed.

Learn B.L.A.S.T.

The 5 Distance Keys to Distance can be remembered by the acronym B.L.A.S.T. It is a perfect mnemonic since you will soon be "blasting" your drives down the fairway. The term B.L.A.S.T. stands for:

Balance

Leverage

Arc Width

Speed of Hip Turn

Target Extension

Each of these B.L.A.S.T. areas is explained in detail. You will understand **What** you are supposed to achieve, **Why** you are trying to achieve it, **How** you should do it, and the **How-To** drills that reinforce execution.

Watching Video And Reading About The Drills

The best way for you to use this book is to read each **Distance Key** section entirely and then watch the drill videos. Some students have found it helpful to watch the videos first, then read about them. After you have reviewed the entire book, go out and try the drills. Once you have tried the drills you will find it helpful to review this material again. Experiment, learn, and above all, have some fun.

You will likely have a number of questions the first time you try the drills. That is natural. Once you have some experience with each drill, I recommend that you peruse the book again and watch each of the videos again. Chances are you will pick up on many fine details that weren't apparent to you the first time you went through the material, and most of your questions will be answered.

The written explanations will give you much more detail about the drills, their purpose, how to perform them, and variations you can use to achieve more results. The videos will demonstrate how to perform the drills with ease and precision. The two media support each other, thus enhancing the learning process.

Reading about a drill is helpful because it is possible to include many nuances, specific sequencing, and the philosophy behind the drill. On the other hand, it is difficult to completely understand how to actually DO a drill by simply reading about it.

That is probably one of the challenges you have experienced when reading about swing tips in golf magazines. Even with graphic illustrations you can get the main thrust of the drill or swing tip. However, you miss the dynamic nature of the concept because the swing is best understood in motion.

I believe the combination of both written explanation and video presentation is ideally suited for learning about golf.

With the addition of video, you can see the dynamic movement. In fact, this combination of written and video media gives you a much greater comprehension of what you are trying to accomplish and why, how to accomplish it, and what to look for when achieving results.

Master Each Distance Key In Order

The ideal way to use this book is to follow the process in the order it is presented. In fact, mastering each step in the order presented is critical to your success.

For instance, your first step is to understand and master Balance. You may be tempted to move on to the second step, Leverage, or the third step, Swing Arc Width, before mastering Balance. If you do, your center contact will suffer, as will your approach angle, and your consistency will go out the window. It's great to hit it over 300 yards, but it is hard to score from the weeds.

So, take the time to study each step, and learn them in the order presented.

At the end of this book I've included a section on how to practice. More than likely you have never been told how to practice effectively before, so this section may open your eyes. If you practice in the manner outlined in this book you will learn much more quickly and efficiently, and your improved swing will be long lasting.

Acknowledgements

I wish to thank the many people who contributed to the creation of this book. Without their help this project would have been impossible to finish. First and foremost, my wonderful wife Maureen, who provided the support, space, and encouragement to get it done. John Rediger, who didn't realize how big an elephant this project would be until after he agreed to join me on the journey. We've both learned a lot about video and then some. Rick Laforet, whose patience, encouragement, and steadfastness are always an inspiration,. Leith Anderson, who wrote the foreword and helped for so many years with the technical analysis of clubs. Pete Wlodkowski, who helped reignite my passion for the golf business. Dr. Glen Albaugh, who has been a mentor and friend, and whose keen insights have been invaluable. Steven Rivera, David Talaber, and Peter Holthe of my guru mastermind group, who ask hard questions and provide great perspective. Vidya Tolani, whose giftedness is only outweighed by her patience. My many students, who have worked so diligently with all these concepts and provided the feedback that allowed me to refine the ideas and drills down to what really works. Thank you one and all.

Forward
by Leith Anderson

When asked why he never found an instructor to help him with his golf swing, Lee Trevino quipped: "Because I never found one who could beat me."

If you are looking for distance, you won't have that problem with Eric Jones. He can drive the ball farther than you—and farther than practically anyone else on the planet. Better yet, he can help **you** gain more distance. You won't waste time "rebuilding your swing." Eric works with the swing you have.

You will be required to gain a technical understanding of the golf swing. The way you contact the ball determines your "launch ballistics"—ball speed, launch angle and spin rate. Eric will show you how to do that.

Eric was one of the very first long drive professionals to employ launch monitor data to perfect his technique. He worked with us testing his equipment relentlessly and discovering the effect on performance of removing a few grams of weight or orienting a shaft in the most stable position. Improvement came in small increments—but added together produced major results, including multiple championship titles.

When it came time to compete, Eric never had a doubt that both his technique and his equipment were as perfect as they could be. That dedication has allowed him to stay competitive against younger and stronger players.

I know Eric's techniques work. For many years he made the trek from Walnut Creek to our shop in Palo Alto where he began the development of his teaching theories working with our clients. I have watched him give hundreds of lessons.

In the early days, we used to offer a guarantee. If a client didn't gain five miles per hour of swing speed in a single lesson with Eric—he didn't pay. That never happened.

Since he won the Re/Max Senior World Long Drive Championship in 2003, Eric has committed to developing his knowledge, professional skills and credentials. He completed his Masters Degree in Sports Psychology. Then, he earned his PGA membership in record time. When he sets a goal, Eric gets the job done.

I have just one word of warning. Simply reading the book will not produce longer drives. After you understand your goals, you will have to set aside the time to practice the drills. True improvement requires hard work. The road map Eric provides is the quickest way to lasting success.

The 5 Keys to Distance is very well organized, remarkably detailed, and easy to understand. When you read it and use the drills I have no doubt you will improve your distance. With its depth of information and the use of written and video instruction, *The 5 Keys to Distance* sets the new standard for golf instructional books.

The improvement process will go faster if you have some professional help. Players who live in the San Francisco Bay Area are lucky: they can work with Eric personally. You need to "see yourself" on video. Your imagination will not tell you that you're on the right path. When it comes time to check your progress scientifically, track down a professional club fitter who can help you fine tune your "launch ballistics" with the right equipment.

The 5 Keys to Distance is a great start on your quest to play better golf. Enjoy the read and enjoy the journey.

Leith Anderson
Clubfitter of the Year
www.calgolftech.com

INTRODUCTION

THE 5 KEYS TO DISTANCE
How To Drive The Golf Ball Farther

Can you really pick up 20 to 50 yards or more off the tee?

Yes, you can, and this book will show you how.

This book is all about DISTANCE: where it comes from and how you can get more of it off the tee and with all your shots.

My name is Eric Jones, MA (Sport Psychology), PGA Professional, and World Long Drive Champion, and I'm going to help you add 20, 30, or even 50 yards or more to your drives.

How?

By giving you everything I learned on the way to winning the most coveted title in Long Drive: The Re/Max World Long Drive Championship and becoming one of the top long drive professionals in the world.

The 5 Keys to Distance is about helping you understand what you need to do to get more distance off the tee: the swing mechanics, the physics, the biomechanics, the mental approach, the practice routines, the drills, and even the learning process. Every lesson I've had to learn the hard way. Every technique I use myself. This is the process my students are using to achieve their own remarkable results. I know this will work for you.

I wish you good luck and great distance!

1

IT'S ALL ABOUT SPEED

First and foremost: Driving it long is all about delivering maximum clubhead speed through the ball at impact. End of story. Anything else is wasted energy.

Achieving Maximum Clubhead Speed

The 5 Keys to Distance is about helping you achieve maximum clubhead speed at impact. Keep this in mind when you start working on the program outlined in this book. Don't do the drills or techniques prescribed just for the technique's sake. Do them to generate clubhead speed. If the drill is working, keep it up, and try the variations.

If the drill isn't working, don't do it. If you have physical issues that prevent you from implementing the drills, please don't create additional issues or harm yourself. I am not an expert in exercise physiology. Use your good judgment and also consult a physician for advice prior to any physical activity.

I encourage you to contact me with your own story. Let me know your results and what you discover. Helping students to achieve their goals is what keeps me passionate about teaching.

1

What You Will Find In This Book

You are about to learn 5 key swing concepts that will allow you to make the most of your physical abilities and hit the ball as far as you are capable of hitting it.

Once you have implemented the drills and practice routines you will have a natural feel for how to generate more clubhead speed. When you read the text and watch the drill videos you will have both the theory and the execution.

You may not perfect it right away. But if you stick with it you'll expand your knowledge and have some fun.

What this book will show you:
1.　What you are supposed to do and when
2.　Why you are supposed to do it
3.　How to do it
4.　Real examples in video supported by written explanations
5.　Specific drills for each step of the progression
6.　How to practice to achieve maximum results in minimum time

2

DEVELOPING AN EXPERTISE IN SPEED

I have a natural talent for hitting it long. Always have. I almost always hit my drives farther than anybody else in my foursome. But hitting it long on Saturday with the boys is not the same as teeing it up with the big boys in long drive. Until I figured out the information you'll find in this book, I was definitely NOT long enough to win the World Long Drive Championship.

When I attended my first local long drive qualifying event I really didn't have a more sophisticated strategy than "grip it and rip it." I had played college golf at Stanford and I was playing a lot of amateur tournament golf. I was ranked in Northern California, and I had spent time helping my friend Pete Wlodkowski launch www.amateurgolf. com, a site dedicated to helping amateur golfers play and compete. At that point in my journey, I was more interested in tournament play than long drive.

Qualifying For The World Championships

But I am a competitor, and when I tee it up I want to win. Although I

3

attended the local long drive qualifier on a lark, when I was on the tee I still wanted to out-drive everybody else. I won that first local long drive event, which qualified me for the District Championships.

I knew the district qualifier would be much more competitive than the local qualifiers, so I got serious about learning how to hit a longer club (50" was the maximum length in 2003). I had a month to get ready for the competition and to learn how to generate more clubhead speed. So I spent that month experimenting with my swing.

I was able to figure out a few things on my own largely through trial and error. With patience, persistence and study, I discovered the techniques that work.

As I expected, the district championship was considerably tougher than the local qualifier. But I advanced through the rounds and earned my spot at the RE/MAX World Long Drive Championships.

While I was elated to have earned that spot, I had a newfound appreciation for the dedication and talent of long drive competitors. I knew I still had plenty of work to do.

Learning To Swing Fast

So I got REALLY serious about maximizing my distance. I got downright *scientific*. I studied. I experimented. I tweaked. I tinkered. I found some good techniques and discarded others.

I collaborated with Leith Anderson (www.calgolftech.com) and measured specific results. I got on the launch monitor and measured everything—clubhead speed, ball speed, smash factor, clubface angle, angle of approach, side spin, backspin, launch angle, and club path. Then we took the clubs apart and rebuilt them to see which variables were most important.

It took time, but when I took those results back to the range I knew what I needed to do to generate and deliver the maximum clubhead speed at impact with a square clubface.

Armed with knowledge I was able to increase my swing speed more than 20 mph, from around 120 mph. to more than 140 mph. That increase added more than 60 yards to my long drives and I was able to maintain my accuracy. I am still known as one of the most accurate hitters in long drive.

What I learned in that six weeks of intensive training helped me capture the 2003 Senior Division World Long Drive Championship title. But I didn't stop there.

What I learned over the course of the next several years helped me to win the 2004 LDA Long Drive Tour Rookie of the Year honors and the 2006 Players Tour Long Drive Championship, where I was the first Senior Long Driver to win both the Open and the Senior Division titles at the same event.

I didn't accomplish these things by being the biggest or strongest guy on the tee. In fact, at 6 feet tall, I am one of the smaller guys out there. I had success because I implemented the concepts outlined in this book.

Now long drivers from all over the west come to see me for help and advice. Equally as important, amateur players and weekend warriors seek me out to help them hit it farther. The lessons and knowledge I learned the hard way helped build a solid foundation for me today, as an instructor/coach assisting players as they achieve the maximum use of their abilities.

Learning As A Lifelong Endeavor

My studies haven't stopped with the technical and mechanical aspects of the clubs. While I was studying the elements of distance I went back to school to obtain my Masters Degree in Sport Psychology from John F. Kennedy University, one of the country's leading institutions in applied sport psychology. I enrolled in the PGA's Professional Golf Management program to learn as much about teaching and instruction as possible, and I achieved my PGA Class A Professional status.

Learning is a lifelong endeavor for me. Learning and sharing are my passions. I humbly mention my credentials to give you an idea of the level of my commitment to being the best golf instructor possible for individuals just like you. I like to tell my students—I'm passionate about people who are passionate about their golf game. If you have passion, then I will commit to helping you in any way I can.

Warning

Some of the things I will tell you and show you in this book may fly in the face of today's modern teaching methods. Here's what I have to say to that: Try it first. If it works and you like it, use it. If it doesn't work, don't use it.

The art of teaching golf is constantly evolving, and what is commonly taught today will change in the future. Some of the concepts in this book may be leading edge at the moment, but common practice tomorrow. I encourage you to keep an open mind and to maintain a willingness to experiment. Regardless of the technique you will still need to find a way to make it work for your own unique swing.

3

THE ELEMENTS OF DISTANCE

I am going to take a moment to give you some technical information. You don't need to memorize this information, but just knowing it may help you practice and learn more efficiently, and being deliberate in your learning will help you to progress much faster.

1. Distance is affected by a combination of three things: speed, center contact, and clubhead angle of approach. Speed is the most important factor by far. Thus, the largest portion of this book is dedicated to helping you find ways to increase your clubhead speed.

2. But speed is not the only thing. And if you want to maximize your distance potential, you need to know the other factors that affect distance—things that are not opinion, but are based on the laws of physics and aerodynamics. You can argue all you want about some of the technique recommendations, but the laws of physics apply to everyone, and for every shot.

3. The second distance factor (after clubhead speed) is Center Contact. Simply translated: this means how well you hit the ball squarely in the middle of the clubface.

4. Here are some basic statistics: A 100 mph swing will drive the ball approximately 240 yards if hit perfectly square. A ball struck ¼ inch off-center will decrease distance 2-3%, or 3-5 yards. A ball struck ½ inch off-center will decrease distance 5%, or 12 yards. A ball struck ¾ inch off center will decrease distance 10-15%, or 25-40 yards*.

5. Ask your local PGA pro for some impact tape. Put it on your clubface and hit some balls. Your impact pattern can be very revealing. How close to the center of the clubface do you routinely hit the ball?

6. The third factor that influences distance is your clubhead's Angle of Approach. A steeper downswing will impart more backspin, which in turn creates more "lift" to the ball. Your ball will go higher, but you will lose distance since some of the kinetic energy imparted to the ball is at an angle to the direction of flight. For this reason you want to hit the drive on a slight upswing to impart ideal backspin rates.

Information courtesy of the PGA of America

A Long Driver's Angle Of Approach

The more closely you can match your angle of approach to the launch angle, the more efficiently you impart energy to the ball and the farther it will go. For instance, if my driver loft is 10 degrees and my ideal launch angle when the ball takes off is 16 degrees, then the ideal angle of approach would be a club ascending to the ball at a 6% angle (6% angle plus 10% face loft—16% launch angle).

For instance, when I am in long drive competitions I typically use a 5% lofted driver. Most clubs used in long drive are 48" in length—the USGA's maximum allowed length. For every inch of driver length above 45" there is a corresponding increase in driver loft at impact of about 1 degree (due to the action on the shaft—sag and deflection). So the net effective loft of my 5 degree driver is about 8 degrees.

My Launch Angle

My ideal launch angle is around 12 to 14 degrees. I know this because I have hit thousands of balls on a launch monitor. That means my ideal swing path is 5 degrees up at the ball.

My spin rate is lower than most, around 2,200 rpm, and this combination produces for me the ideal trajectory PLUS roll-out/release when the ball lands. That is one of the reasons most long drivers tee the ball up higher than normal. They are using a lower lofted club to reduce the amount of backspin, and compensating for the lower launch angle by swinging up slightly more during the swing.

A 14 degree launch angle is not ideal for wet conditions. When the ground is wet, I need to increase my launch angle to 16-18 degrees to get the best combination of air time/roll-out. I usually tee the ball up a little higher (only about ½ inch), and move the ball slightly forward (only about ¾ inch) to get a little more air time.

Shallowing Out Your Swing

How much is a 4 or 5 degree angle of approach? Not much.

If you laid a standard 45" driver on the ground and put a golf ball under the end of the grip you would be at about 4 degrees. That is why the swing is generally described as a "U" shaped swing rather than a "V" shaped swing.

What this means is that you don't have to start making big adjustments in your swing by swinging more upward. In fact, the opposite is probably true. The average golfer probably has too high of an entry and exit angle (the "V" swing), and most people need to think more about shallowing out their swings to get closer to a "U" shape.

Your Launch Angle

For the average golfer, the ideal launch angle is between 16 degrees and 20 degrees. Average golfers need to maximize their air time rather than optimize trajectory for roll-out. Generally the slower the swing speed, the higher the launch angle needs to be, so carry distance can be maximized.

The need for more air time is one of the reasons some people tee it up higher. It is also one of the reasons seniors and ladies typically play with a higher lofted driver. The air provides significantly less friction/resistance than the ground. If your ball travels 10% farther on the ground once it hits you'd be doing well. That means for a 240-yard drive, if you got another 20-25 yards of roll you'd be pleased.

In summary, there are three elements of distance: clubhead speed, center contact, and angle of approach. As stated, the most important by far is speed.

Ball Flight

Just a little more technical information on ball flight. The **direction** the ball travels is determined by the club **path** (straight, left/pull, right/push) while the **shape** of the shot (straight, slice, hook) is determined by the **face angle**, which produces side spin. Thus, a straight golf shot is a square path and a square face.

If you had a weight on the end of a string and you imagined it swinging back and forth like a pendulum you could easily imagine a straight-back, straight-through path. If you could tilt the string to match the angle of your club shaft at address and somehow manipulate gravity so the weight would still swing straight back and forth the same way, you would have a straight-back, straight-through club path. To someone standing behind the weight the path would look like an arc.

Swing Path And Ball Flight

There are three possible swing paths: straight, outside-in (right to left), and inside-out (left to right). There are only 3 possible ball flights: straight, slice (left to right), and hook (right to left). If you put the two together, you have 9 possible shots depending on the path of the club and the angle of the clubface.

Ball Path 1: Straight Shots
   a.   Straight—Square/square (square path, square face angle)
   b.   Pull—A straight shot to the left. Outside-in path/square face.
   c.   Push—A Straight shot to the right. Inside-out path/square face.

(Notice that the first three shot patterns all describe a **straight** ball flight. The club **face** is square in each. The only variable is the club **path**, which affects the direction).

Ball Path 2: Fade/Slice Shots
   a.   Slice—The ball starts out straight toward the target, but curves to the right. Square path/open face
   b.   Pull-Slice—The ball starts out left of the target and curves right back toward the target. Outside-in path/open face
   c.   Push-Slice—The ball starts out going right and then curves even more to the right. Inside-out path/open face

(Notice again in all three slice examples the **face** is the same—open— but the **path** is different).

Ball Path 3: Draw/Hook Shots
   a.   Draw—square path/closed face
   b.   Pull-draw—outside-in path/closed face
   c.   Push-draw—inside-out path/closed face

(Notice that with a draw the club face is closed, and the only variable is the swing path. A closed face at impact will impart the kind of sidespin that will make the ball travel right to left).

Why do I take the time to describe the shot patterns? If you are trying to fix a slice by adjusting your swing path you are in for a frustrating effort. You are addressing the wrong issue. A slice is caused by an open club face at impact. You need to address the swing issues that cause the face angle change.

Hitting The Shot You Want
Similarly, if you are trying to *achieve* a particular shot—and most of my students would love to hit a little draw with the drive (technically

a slight push-draw—a shot that starts out down the right center of the fairway and draws back 5-10 yards to the center), then you know you need a slightly inside-out swing (to achieve the push path) with a slightly closed club face at impact (for the draw action).

Notice I said "slight." 1 or 2 degrees here is all you'll need. Often students think that if a little is good, a lot must be even better. Not true! Keep it in moderation, and have it occur as naturally as possible.

I'm interested in studying ball flight laws and the laws of physics because I know that if I concentrate on refining and maximizing the physical components of the swing (as they relate to the laws of physics), I can help my students maximize distance.

The point of this information is not to supplant the "eye" and knowledge of a trained professional. The point is to give you a foundational understanding of the elements that really contribute to distance and accuracy. This knowledge will allow you to apply the concepts to your own unique circumstance to develop a solution that works best for you.

4

UNDERSTANDING THE ROLE OF SELF-AWARENESS IN LEARNING

Making permanent, long-term positive progress in your golf game is a process that involves increasing your awareness of what your body is doing and what it should be doing. If you can't feel it, you won't be aware of it. If you are not aware of it, you can't improve it. It is worth taking a moment to discuss the process you will experience as you refine your swing, so you will understand where you are in the process as well as how to evaluate your progress.

Develop Your Self-Awareness And Feedback Systems

Developing a highly refined self-awareness and feedback system is key to helping you pick up more distance. It is also going to be one of the significant side-benefits for your entire game once you've completed this book and the accompanying drills.

Developing your feedback system and awareness will help you to understand your swing better (in all conditions), and you will ultimately have a lot more confidence in your swing because you will be shaping it deliberately.

Having a more refined feedback and awareness system will also help with consistency, scoring clubs, chipping, and putting. In fact, this concept is so important that I cover it in all of the instructional material I develop. Getting a head start on it now will help you move that much faster to improve the rest of your game.

There is considerably more information on effective practice available in **The Practice Effect:** *How To Groove A Reliable, Automatic Swing You Can Trust.* I invite you to learn more about the book, co-authored with fellow PGA Professional John Snopkowski, at www.targetcenteredgolf.com

Focus On The Feedback, Not The Results

The message is this: your initial practice should be focused on developing your awareness, not on hitting long bombs. The long shots will come. The actual outcome of the shot doesn't matter as much as your ability to feel and understand what is happening. Refining your swing for speed is a two-part process: First is self-awareness and second is self-regulation.

The reason I spend time on this concept early in the book (when I know you are itching to get to the drills), is that by focusing on the idea of developing your self-awareness and feedback system and keeping this idea in the back of your mind while you learn each step and the drills, you can be formulating a practice plan in your subconscious. It will make learning much more enjoyable, and you will be much more efficient in your practice. The end result is that you will be more persistent because you will be less interested in the outcome of the shot and more interested in whether you can feel what you are attempting to accomplish in that swing.

Recognizing progress in your ability to sense or feel something in your swing is just as important as getting progressively better at a drill. In fact, it is a necessary precursor to getting better at a drill and ultimately making the swing refinements you want to achieve.

The Three Stages Of Learning

When we learn a new skill we typically progress through three stages of learning. Learning to recognize these stages will help you measure and understand your progress and move through the stages faster.

The **first** stage of learning is the **Cognitive Stage**. In the Cognitive learning stage you will be consciously thinking and sensing every part of your swing and every refinement you are making. Your higher brain—your neocortex—is actively engaged in the process. Because you are actively thinking of each part of the swing your motion will tend to be jerky and somewhat uncoordinated.

The **second** stage of learning is the **Associative or Integrative Stage**. In the Integrative stage those discrete steps that you were consciously thinking about during the cognitive stage start to get grouped together into larger and larger components. Your motion is still not completely smooth, but parts of the swing become smoother and your performance improves. We spend most of our time on the practice range in the Integrative stage of learning.

The **third** stage of learning is the **Automatic Stage**. In the Automatic stage your motion is smooth and effortless. Your action is automatic, which is to say it is completed without conscious thought. We play our best golf, and get the most distance, when allowing our swing to happen automatically. Perhaps you have experienced the sensation of being "in the zone" when playing. Automaticity is a key feature of being in the zone.

You should aspire in your practice to be as automatic as possible. We don't spend enough of our time on the range practicing being automatic—in other words, just letting the swing happen. Consider reserving some portion of your practice time to allowing your swing to be automatic and see what happens. It will be a good test to see which of the drills and techniques you have mastered.

As you learn each of **The 5 Keys to Distance**, your goal is to progress through the three stages of learning as rapidly as possible, until effortless distance is automatic. It will take some time, however, as well as some practice. There is simply no getting around this fact. There is a process your brain and body have to follow in order to learn even simple skills like walking.

Learning Is A Positive Experience

Understanding the process as well as how you are progressing can inform one of the most important weapons in your bag—your positive mental attitude.

As you are learning, you will be refining your swing for speed. Not every shot you hit will be perfect. Far from it. I would like to reinforce the notion that it is critical for your positive attitude that you resist the temptation to judge your shots when you are learning. Avoid using words like good or bad when you are practicing. There are no good or bad shots when you are practicing—only information.

Instead, use descriptive words like left, right, high, low, open club face, outside-in swing, etc. These terms represent useful, practical data. Words like good and bad are subjective, they don't carry much valuable data, and they have a distinct emotional overtone that can lead to frustration instead of learning. Keep your judgment neutral to keep your thought process positive. You will learn much faster and your learning experience will be much more enjoyable. With a non-judgmental approach, you will find it easier to build a repeatable swing that generates effortless distance.

In the next section we'll talk about the biological building blocks necessary for grooving your repeatable swing.

The Myelin Express

When you begin to repeat a motion, your body looks for ways to optimize the motion—to make it more efficient and effective.

One of the ways it does this is to reinforce the neural pathways that create the motion. The more the movement is repeated, the more the neurons are optimized. To optimize electrical signal strength the body uses a substance called myelin, discovered in 1854 by Rudolf Virshow, a German doctor, anthropologist, pathologist and biologist.

Myelin is a naturally-occurring substance composed primarily of fatty tissue. It is found wrapped around nerve cells throughout the body. Although technically white in color, it is what we call "gray matter" when we see a picture of the brain.

During the last few decades research scientists from England, Germany, Canada and the United States have learned a lot more about what happens in the brain and body when people develop, learn and age. In particular, scientists have used brain imaging and other scientific methodologies to show that when people learn a new skill, white matter in the brain increases. That increase in white matter is due to myelination.

Myelin acts like an electrical insulator, increasing the strength of electrical signals. The more a physical movement gets repeated, the more myelin gets wrapped around the specific neurons used to create that motion. Specifically, the myelin layer serves to increase the speed at which impulses move along myelinated neurons.

The stronger the electrical signal along the neural pathways, the more optimized the physical movement associated with those pathways becomes. And the easier it is to repeat the motion. When a certain set of neurons become super-insulated for a specific motion, that motion is more likely than any other to emerge when you swing a golf club, for example.

But neurons don't get myelinated by themselves.

When you think about a particular motion and/or actually create the motion, you fire a specific set of neurons, which in turn activates them. When neurons are activated myelin begins to encircle them, little by little, layer by layer.

It's the little by little, layer by layer part that is important.

You have to keep repeating the motion in order to keep firing the neurons. Firing the neurons leads to more myelination. More myelination improves signal strength, which in turn makes the motion easier and more automatic.

You may have heard an old adage that it takes 21 days to form a new habit. It may be that the adage has its root in the biological process of myelination. Whatever the root of the adage, the fact remains: it is important to stick with your practice, even during times when it seems as if you are not making progress.

This is also why smart practice is so important to making a swing refinement become automatic.

When you focus, deliberately, on making the correct motion, your brain gets busy reinforcing the neural impulses that make the correct motion easier to repeat. Over time your brain will optimize the move by creating a superhighway of myelinated neurons. The end result is that the new or refined motion will become your normal, reliable golf swing.

If you learn the 5 distance keys in order, using the drills associated with each key, you will literally "groove" the distance you want, automatically.

Now that you have some basic understanding of how you will be grooving your new swing refinements, let's tee it up!

5

DISTANCE KEY #1: BALANCE

Balance is one of the most important elements of a consistent and powerful golf swing

I honestly don't know why more teaching professionals aren't spending more time on it with their students. Forget swing plane, x-factors, or holding lag. It doesn't matter what I tell you to do mechanically. If you are out of balance in your swing you will not hit consistent golf shots, and you will not be making the best use of your athleticism to get additional distance.

When you finish your shot and find yourself leaning back, falling forward, falling inward, or taking a step, you are out of balance. You have a major power leak. It is important to fix the balance issue first before making any additional mechanical refinements.

Being out of balance nearly always has negative consequences for the swing, both in terms of inefficiently used energy as well as inconsistency. Just as important, many swing flaws can be traced back to balance. You may be fighting an over-the-top move, thinking it is the primary cause of your erratic ball flight pattern, when in fact it may be a symptom of poor balance. In this case, the over-the-top move is your compensation for lack of athletic balance.

Balance Is A Root Fundamental

When lack of balance causes a swing fault, we say balance is the **root** issue or underlying cause. Whenever you are making any swing improvements, focus on treating the root issue, not the symptom. Treating the symptom is a band-aid fix, and, unfortunately, it is exactly the type of quick fix that you'll sometimes find in golf help magazines and TV shows.

Band-aid fixes do not last, which is why you may have experienced some frustration in the past when you tried a hot new tip, found that it worked for a little while, and then stopped working.

The material in this book deals with root fundamentals. Once you learn them, they won't fade away. Once you learn how to generate more clubhead speed, you will permanently have more distance.

So this is where we start. Learn balance first. You cannot attain your maximum swing speed if you are out of balance during your swing. You must be in an athletic position to deliver fast clubhead speed, and being in an athletic position means being in athletic balance.

Athletic Balance

Allow me to clarify what I mean when I refer to balance. When I use the term balance in the remainder of this book, I am not just referring to the ability to merely remain standing before, during, or after a golf shot. I am really referring to "athletic" balance.

Let me be specific about what I mean by "athletic balance."

In almost any open-skill sport like football, baseball, basketball, or skiing there is a "ready" position that puts you in your most athletic posture to perform. From this position you are "ready" to react. You can move in any direction and respond instantly to the situation. Often you are not even aware of the balance adjustments your body is making when you move. Your body is moving automatically and efficiently to put you in the best position to execute whatever your mind is focused on achieving.

So it is with golf.

An athletic posture or ready position has you in a posture with your knees slightly flexed and your center of mass positioned directly over the balls of your feet. In this position you are capable of moving in any direction. You are athletically "ready." You have "centered balance." Whether your club is on the ground or in the air, your balance is independent and remains unaffected by your club position.

I hope that you have experienced this sense of balance, because it is critical to your success. It is a key foundational concept. You have to get this right in order to allow your body to make its most athletic move. You will not be able to generate your maximum core rotation, and do it consistently, if you don't understand centered balance.

Balance And Your "Center Of Mass"

Your center of mass is generally thought of as a spot a couple of inches above your belly button and a couple of inches in front of your spine.

Here is a way for you to experience centered balance. Imagine you are a basketball player and you are going to jump up to grab a rebound. You bend your knees to gather some force in your legs and then align your center of mass with the direction you want to jump.

If you are jumping straight up, you will automatically center your weight directly over the balls of your feet. If you want to jump forward, you will position your center of mass forward of the balls of your feet. To jump backwards, you will position your center of mass in back of the balls of your feet.

You can picture the relationship between the balls of your feet and your center of mass as a straight vertical line or an axis. The most stable position for that axis is straight up and down. If you make a golf swing with your axis in a stable vertical orientation you will remain in good balance. If you tilt the axis forward at address or during the swing your body will try to make compensations during the swing to return the axis to a stable, vertical position.

Most Golfers Are Out Of Balance

Almost 90% of my students first come to me with their center of mass too far forward—out over their toes. It's not their fault they are out of balance. For the most part, nobody has ever explained the importance of balance. Some students even have to lean on their club at address to remain standing. If they were at the address position and I were to suddenly remove the club, they would fall forward toward the ball! When I ask them to get into their address position and then hop (without re-setting their weight) most of them hop forward. Try it for yourself.

If you are in the correct, athletically centered balance position at address and you hop, you should hop straight up and come straight down. And you should still be in balance when you land. Put the book aside for a moment, grab a club and get in your address position. Then hop.

If you hop forward, try it again. If you hopped straight up down you are in the correct athletically centered balance position. If you made a slight adjustment to your weight just before you jumped try it again and pay attention to any adjustments your body may be making before you hop.

Balance Adjustments

Do your hips rock back slightly? Do your shoulders move slightly back or slightly up? Do you straighten up your spine before you hop?

Some students are already centered, but they are in the minority. Most students have to make at least one adjustment to their hips, shoulders, or spine before they get into an athletically centered position. About half of my students make all three adjustments when they hop.

When I point out the adjustments they are making, students are usually not aware of them. They make the decision to hop and then let their body figure out how to make it happen.

But when they focus their attention on it, without consciously manipulating their set-up position, they are often able to feel their body making adjustments right away. By focusing on their balance as they make more hops they can feel each part of their body lining up in the correct position. Once students understand the adjustments they are making automatically, it is a relatively simple next step to get them to make those same adjustments prior to hitting the ball, and then to stay in that position to make the golf swing. It is more natural for us to be in balance than to be out of balance, so the adjustments feel comfortable right away.

Hip Adjustments

The first adjustment is usually the hips. When students focus on their hips while they get set to jump from their address position, they can usually feel their hips rock back slightly to line up over the balls of their feet. It is an instinctive adjustment. They may move their hips as little as a half-inch to as much as several inches. It is the most common adjustment made by students and one that nearly all players need to make. The adjustment may also involve flattening out the belt angle, or the forward tilt of the pelvis. That is usually a great additional adjustment for people with back issues.

Most of the time, the hip adjustment is sufficient to create an athletically centered stance. Students report almost unanimously that their swing immediately feels freer and more athletic when they are in this posture. Their turn feels better, as does their release. The ball almost always goes farther as well. It is a small but dramatic change. Students can almost always take it to the course and see immediate improvement in their shot making, without it interfering with their normal swing thoughts.

Shoulder Adjustments

The next type of adjustment I often see is a shoulder adjustment. It is a little more subtle, but it can be as dramatic as the hip adjustments in producing a freer swing and more distance.

When students assume their address position and focus on getting set to jump, they instinctively align their shoulders over their hips and move their shoulders back and down. This action centers their weight over the balls of their feet, and it is the only position that will allow them to hop straight up and down.

Try it the wrong way once to get a feel for the difference. Get into your golf address position, hunch your shoulders forward (as though you are trying to touch your elbows together), and hop. You'll hop forward. You'll also notice that this hunched over posture is not very comfortable or athletic.

Now try the same jump in the correct athletic balance with your shoulders open (like you are trying to pinch your shoulder blades together and stick out your chest). It is a much more natural and athletic feel. If you can feel the difference between the two positions, take your normal address position with a club in your hands and get ready to jump. Do you feel your shoulders move back and down just before you hop? If so, then consider getting yourself into that position at address. Chest out. Shoulders back and down.

Spine Adjustments

The third adjustment I often see (and encourage) is when students straighten and lengthen their spine.

Try getting into your address position again and get ready to jump. Pay particular attention this time to your spine. Many students can feel their spine straighten out just before a jump. Their back gets longer. It is a more natural, athletic position. It is a more stable, protected position for the spine that can help avoid back injuries from the long term wear and tear of golf swings.

It is very common for me to see students take their address position by bending at the waist, rather than the hips. Bending from the waist nearly always results in a rounded spine. While this may be a comfortable position at address, the rounded spine often leads to multiple issues during the swing. It is not your most athletic posture.

It is far more beneficial for the player to have a straight spine, since that is the axis around which your entire swing rotates. With a rounded spine you actually set yourself up with two different spine angles, and it is anybody's guess which one you will use as your rotational axis—which means it is anyone's guess as to where the ball will go.

Instead, address the ball. Stand up straight and lock your knees so your legs are straight. This will help you to bend down to the ball from your hips, instead of from your waist, with a straight spine. When the club is grounded behind the ball flex the knees to get into your athletic posture. If you can tap your toes in this posture, you should be athletically centered. You'll see more on the toe tap drill as you read on.

You want to keep yourself in good athletic balance throughout the swing. This means keeping your center of mass positioned over the balls of your feet throughout the swing.

Balance Issues In The Swing

One of the common issues that results from allowing your center of balance to move too far forward—either at address or during the backswing—is that your hips will compensate by moving underneath your center of mass on the downswing. That usually means your hips will move inward toward the ball on the downswing, changing your spine angle. If you were to see a video of your swing and pause it at impact you would see that your spine will curve, your arms will move in closer to your body, your hands will rise up compared to their start position, and your hips may stop rotating. All of these symptoms derive from the loss of athletic balance and will result in inconsistent ball striking and a loss of power at impact.

Now, let's talk about that toe tap drill.

The Simple Balance Check—Happy Toes

This is a very simple way to get into an athletically balanced posture prior to the swing and to see if you are truly in an athletically balanced position. It is also a great step to add into your pre-shot routine and one that I would encourage you to implement right away.

Simply take your stance over the ball with club in hand. Then, lift your club just barely off the ground and tap your toes one at a time. If you can't lift your toes at all when you are at address, your center of mass is too far forward. If you can lift both toes off the ground at the same time, your weight is too far back. You need to find a balance in between these extremes where you can only tap one foot at a time. That should put your center of mass directly over the balls of your feet. That is your action position.

Once you find your athletically centered balance point, be careful to get the clubhead back to the ball without changing your posture. Keep your athletic balance once you have it. Either drop the club into position or extend your left arm to get the club back down to the ball. Do not bend forward.

If you cannot do this easily, try the happy toes process again, but move closer to the ball before you begin to tap your toes. In any case, don't change your upper body posture or your weight position once you have established your athletically balanced address position by tapping your toes.

This simple happy toes exercise serves two purposes. It is not only the first step in helping you make a more athletically centered and balanced swing, it is also the first step in working on your self-awareness and feedback system. When you do this simple drill you will become more aware of how your body is positioned and more aware of the subtle adjustments you need to make in order to make more athletic swings.

Pay attention to this learning process, not just to the act of getting into a more balanced posture. I'll talk more about this later, but for now let me just say this: often highly productive drill practice means being able to consistently tell the difference between one swing and the next, even if the ball flight looks exactly the same on both shots.

Select the "Balance" section on the main menu of the accompanying DVD to view the Happy Toes drill. Or you can find the drill online at: http://www.targetcenteredgolf.com/videos/happy_toes.html

Drill Format: What To Look For

Let me take just a moment to explain what I will be sharing with you for each drill.

Name

With each drill you will get the Name of the drill. For instance, the name of the first drill you will see in the Balance section is what we call the "tight ankles" drill.

Purpose

Next, I will tell you the Purpose of the drill—what you are trying to learn from that specific drill. Please note that the purpose of any given drill is NOT to hit perfect golf shots. As you read on, you'll get a clearer understanding of this. In the case of Tight Ankles, the Purpose is to learn to make a full weight shift while staying in balance.

Short Description

You will then see a short description of the drill—a condensed version that will have all the key elements you need to remember for the drill without the philosophy and detailed discussion of the intent of the drill. The short descriptions will be grouped again at the end of the book so you can copy the pages and bring them with you to the range or paste them in a notebook (recommended!).

Swing Thought

I will also give you a specific Swing Thought to use for focus on the drill. In the case of tight ankles, your Swing Thought will be "solid left side." Keep this single swing thought running through your mind as you perform your drill. It will help you stay focused on what you are attempting to accomplish.

Detailed Drill Description

After the short summary you will then get a much longer description with detailed instructions of how the drill should work and what you should be attempting to accomplish. The long description will contain technique and theory, as well as right ways and wrong ways to perform the drill.

Variations

You will also get some variations on the drill to help you work on other aspects of your swing. These variations should be used once you have mastered the basic drill. They allow you to extend your repertoire and to combine elements to help groove the particular B.L.A.S.T. key the drill is reinforcing.

What The Drills Will—And Won't—Give You

I've already mentioned that the purpose of any given drill is NOT to hit perfect golf shots. Let me explain.

By their nature, drills are designed to work on one particular aspect of the swing. They are to help you achieve a particular motion in the swing. They are also designed to help you increase your self-awareness and your feedback system.

Generally, they are not designed to be an exact replication of the swing. They are also generally not designed to help you hit perfect golf shots.

Rather, drills are an exaggeration of a component of the swing or of a movement. That exaggeration will make it easier for you to feel what you should be doing compared to what you are currently doing. Once again, if you are not aware of what you are doing versus what you should be doing, you won't be able to make refinements.

The drill is not the swing. And it is not the way you will be making your normal golf swing. The way the drill *feels*, however, is something you want to incorporate into your swing.

Remember, your goal when you practice these drills is to improve your self-awareness and feedback system. Once you are aware of something, only then can you work to improve or refine a particular aspect of your swing.

Balance Drills

Here are the drills related to balance. To view them, select "Balance" on the main menu of the accompanying DVD.

Balance Drill #1: Tight Ankles
Balance Drill #2: Baseball Rip Swing
Balance Drill #3: Toe Tap

Balance Drill #1: Tight Ankles.

Purpose

Learn about BALANCE while swinging with a full weight shift.

Swing Thought

"Solid Left Side"

Short Description

Stand with your feet together (ankles tight together). On the backswing lift the heel of the left foot off the ground (keeping your toe in contact with the ground) and transfer all of your weight to your right foot. On the downswing shift your weight from your right foot to your left, allowing your right heel to come up. This action is just like walking in place. Swing the club through and hit the ball with your ankles together. Hold your finish position for 3 seconds. Your goal is to make a complete weight transfer while hitting a ball and finishing your swing with no wobble or balance issues. Don't watch the ball. Instead, feel where your weight is at impact. You should feel your weight at impact toward the outside part of your left foot, centered down through your left ankle.

Detailed Description Tight Ankles Drill

I usually encourage students to master this simple drill in a series of steps, gradually adding components.

Step One: Walk In Place

First, put your feet together and simply stand upright without a club. While keeping your toes in contact with the ground, lift your heels to mimic walking in place while shifting your weight from one foot to the other. Since we all walk every day, this part of the exercise is pretty straight forward. You aren't swinging a club yet, so you should be in a normal posture for walking. Keep your toes in contact with the ground and march in place.

If you are fortunate enough to have a sunny day, toss a ball in front of you and stand with your back to the sun so the ball is within the shadow of your head. Begin to walk in place, doing the tight ankles drill, keeping your toes on the ground and shifting your weight back and forth.

Pay attention to the way the shadow of your head moves. Your goal is to keep your shadow stationary on the ball. That is, your shadow doesn't move as you swing and shift your weight. If you notice your head moving back and forth while you lift your heels and transfer your weight, try to stabilize your upper body so your shadow always covers the ball. If your head is moving back and forth or up and down, you have already identified one of the consistency issues in your swing.

Step Two: Swing A Club Gently, In Rhythm

Add a club and swing it gently back and forth as you walk in place (we are not hitting a ball yet). A gentle swing is one in which you keep your hands below your waist.

Swing the club a foot or so above the ground. There is no need to be in a golf stance position just yet, and no need to brush the grass. You are feeling your weight shift and establishing a rhythm with this drill, so you want to keep the club moving back and forth continuously while you are shifting your weight and lifting your heels—all the while remaining in balance.

Keep your eye on the shadow of your head and the ball within the shadow as you swing the club back and forth. Again your goal is to achieve a complete weight transfer while remaining in balance. No wobble, tilting, or steps. If you see your head moving back and forth, make adjustments to your swing until you can stay in complete balance throughout the swing and your upper body movement stabilizes. The ball should stay easily within the boundaries of your shadow.

Experiment with your weight position and your posture as you swing the club back and forth. Stand taller by straightening you spine and move your weight back and forth on your feet. Try to get a feel for your most stable posture and weight position. You will nearly always find that your most stable position is when your center of mass is directly over the center of your feet.

Once you feel that centered position, remember it and what it feels like. Also remember the adjustments you made to get in that position.

Gradually increase the length of your swing to make as full a swing as is comfortable while still maintaining balance. When you are comfortable swinging the club back and forth while maintaining balance and the golf ball is staying within the bounds of your shadow, you are ready to hit a ball.

Step Three: Hit A Ball

Start with your feet tight together. Put a ball down and place the club behind it at address. You may find you need to stand a little closer than normal to easily reach the ball. Set your balance over the center of your feet before you swing. You should feel athletically balanced with your center of mass over the balls of your feet.

As you take your backswing lift your left heel and transfer your weight to your right foot. You should be able to get almost 100% of your weight on your right foot. You only need to hit the ball 20 to 30 yards, so you do not need a big backswing with this drill. In fact, it is usually better to start out with very small swings (keep you hands below your waist like a short chip shot) until you get a feel for the drill.

Minimize Hip Turn

There is very little hip rotation in this drill, so you won't be turning your core far away from the ball. Instead, keep your motion similar to the movement you were making when you were just walking in place. Knees bending straight forward, posture relatively upright.

You may wind up with more of an arm swing at first due to the lack of core rotation. That is ok. Remember, you are only focusing on one thing—the ability to make a full weight transfer while staying in balance. This is not a replica of your normal swing. It is a drill to help you feel and understand balance.

Think Solid Left Side

Start your downswing by planting your left heel and transferring your weight to your left side. At the same time, allow your right heel to come up off the ground. Your only thought during the swing should be "solid left side." This swing thought should help you finish the swing without any wobble, lean, or extra steps.

There is very little forward hip rotation or core turn in the follow through. When you finish your swing and hit the ball, you should still be more or less facing the spot on the ground where the ball was resting.

Hold Your Finish

Finish your swing and hold your finish for a count of at least three.

Pay attention to any wobble or difficulty you may have in retaining your balance.

If you have a balance issue in your swing, it will more than likely show up right away in this Tight Ankles drill. If you fall backward, inward or have to take a step to maintain your balance, odds are that the same issue causing the imbalance during the drill is occurring in your normal swing.

Feel Your Weight—Don't Look

I also recommend that you don't look up to see where the ball is going, especially when you are first doing this drill. After all, you are only hitting a 20- to 30-yard shot, which should be a very short swing.

The first reason I make this recommendation is because it is easier to maintain your balance if you don't look up.

The second reason I suggest not looking up at the ball is to keep your focus on the appropriate things—your balance and your internal awareness of what is happening to your balance during the dynamic swing.

When you look up your focus shifts to the ball and an analysis of what it is doing, and therefore shifts away from what you are feeling. Instead, you should be paying attention to what your weight shift felt like during the swing, where your weight was at impact, and where your weight is at the finish.

We humans are visual processing animals. A large portion of our brain is dedicated to analyzing visual input. When you look up to see where the ball is going you very quickly lose your kinesthetic sense of where your balance was during the swing. You also quickly forget what you were thinking about during the swing. Remember, your single swing thought during the drill is solid left side. You are working on your self-awareness and feedback capabilities.

If you do this drill correctly you should end up with virtually 100% of your weight comfortably on your left foot, without any wobble, lean, or steps. You should feel your weight centered over your left foot, with your center of mass directly over your left ankle.

Finish Position

It is possible you have never paid much attention to the way you automatically center your balance point (your center of mass) over your feet. When standing you naturally stabilize your center of mass over your ankles. It is the most efficient way to stand. Try the following exercise:

Stand up for a moment in a comfortable position. Close your eyes and concentrate on how your weight feels through your feet. Experiment a bit by moving your upper body (and therefore your center of mass) forward and backward, or even to the side. Concentrate on feeling your weight through your feet. If you keep your eyes closed during this exercise you will quickly feel that your most comfortable, natural, stable position occurs when you center your weight over your ankles.

You should feel your weight in the same place when you are finished with your tight ankles drill—centered through your left ankle.

Common Balance-Related Swing Issues

The most common balance issue I see is with the weight too far forward over the toes. When you do the tight ankles drill incorrectly your weight at impact will be up on your toes or on the wide part of your foot. This position nearly always results in a wobbly finish or a step inward, especially as you try to hold your finish for 3 seconds.

To address this issue start your swing with your weight more centered over the balls of your feet, or concentrate on keeping your center of mass over the middle of your feet during the swing. You should finish with your weight centered over your left ankle.

The second most common issue is leaving too much weight on the back (right) foot at impact. This may be the result of not making a weight shift at all or of the upper body moving backward on the downswing. In either case you wind up with weight on the back foot or you make a step backward as you try to hold your finish. It is more than likely that the same issue that shows up in your normal golf swing. This lack of weight shift or backward movement of the upper body through impact is a significant power loss.

Try a few easy swings at first. Gradually make the swings bigger until you can practically make a full shoulder turn with your feet together and still remain in balance. It may take you a week or so of consistent 5-ball sets of tight ankles to work up to big swings. A successful practice set is when you can hit five consecutive Tight Ankles shots without any wobble at the finish.

Adding More Training Elements To Tight Ankles

As you are doing this gentle club swinging/walking you can add a few elements when you are comfortable. Add these elements only after you have mastered the basic drill.

Variation 1 Tight Ankles: Straight Left Arm

Keep your left elbow straight as you swing back and forth, making relatively short swings. You may notice that keeping your elbow straight will necessitate more shoulder action as well as more core body rotation. This core rotation will help to generate more clubhead speed in later drills, and the straight left elbow will contribute significantly to a wider arc as well as more consistent ball striking.

If the straight left elbow results in an increase in upper body sway or loss of balance, shorten up the swing until you can complete the swings comfortably. Gradually lengthen the swing as you gain mastery.

Variation 2 Tight Ankles: Flat Left Wrist

As you are making the tight ankles swings you can also focus on keeping the left wrist flat throughout the swing, particularly at impact and through to the finish. Practicing a flat left wrist will help achieve a better feel for the hand position at impact. It will necessitate more forearm rotation to keep the wrist flat, and this rotation will be beneficial in later drills to help keep the clubface square at impact.

Avoid cupping or flipping the wrist, particularly at impact or after impact. You want to learn to rotate the forearms, not flip the club. You also want to learn to have a nice, firm left hand and left wrist at impact.

Keeping a focus on a flat wrist and a firm left hand through impact will also help to eliminate right hand domination—another significant swing problem for many people and a major power loss. Your right hand should be along for the ride, not doing the majority of the work.

Variation 3 Tight Ankles: Right Foot Pick-up

A third element you can add to double check your weight position and ultimate balance is to pick up your right foot entirely off the ground once the swing is finished. With a little bit of practice you will be able to accomplish this position effortlessly. Give yourself a full second after you have hit the ball to finish your swing and complete your weight shift, then pick up your right foot. You should still be in balance and you should be able to lift your right foot easily.

Variation 4 Tight Ankles: Full Swing Integration

In all likelihood you will find an immediate improvement in your ball striking when you master your balance. But the Tight Ankles drill is a significant departure from your normal swing because your feet are so close together. To begin to integrate the balanced feel of the Tight Ankles drill with the full swing, try shifting to a 3-ball process with a half-step (with feet 6 inches apart) between the Tight Ankles drill and the full swing.

Start with 3 balls. **Ball #1:** With the first ball hit a Tight Ankles drill. **Ball #2:** With the second ball take a half-stance (feet approximately 6 inches apart), and otherwise repeat the Tight Ankles drill. Each time mimic the walking-in-place motion by lifting the left heel on the backswing and shifting all your weight to the right foot. Then reverse the process for the down swing.

Again, your only swing thought should be balance on that solid left side. You will find that with a half-stance you almost automatically turn more, both on the backswing and on the follow through, although it won't be as much as a full swing.

Ball #3: With the third ball take a normal, full swing. Allow your body to move as naturally and athletically as possible. Your only swing thought is balance on that solid left side. Hold your finish position for at least 3 seconds to check your true balance. Repeat these 3-ball sets as often as necessary.

The more you practice these drills the easier it will be to feel and evaluate any differences between the drill and the full swing. Remember, you are working on developing your self-awareness and feedback system.

Compare The Drill To Your Full Swing

Any drill that allows you to compare the feel of the drill with the feel of the full swing is an excellent mechanism for comparing and contrasting. The faster you hone your ability to understand the differences between your current swing and your refined swing the faster you will learn.

This process of adopting a half-step between the drill and the full swing is also a good integration strategy whenever you want to make a mechanical refinement. You can use this half-step integration strategy with all the drills as a way to work them into your full swing.

A Side Note On The Tight Ankles Drill

I use the tight ankles drill when I first get to the driving range to warm up. If I am headed to the golf course to play and I don't have time to hit practice balls or if there is no range facility, I spend 3-4 minutes swinging back and forth with a tight ankles stance. It is a great way to establish both rhythm and balance, and to get the muscles loosened up to play.

Select "Balance" on the main menu of the accompanying DVD to view the video of the Tight Ankles drill. Or you can find the drill at: http://www.targetcenteredgolf.com/videos/tight_ankles.html

Balance Drill #2: Baseball Swing with Rip Swing (warm up)

Purpose

To Practice a full hip turn and learn to swing with speed while staying in balance.

Turn (the hips). Rip it!

These pictures show the baseball rip sequence. Make a series of continuous back and forth baseball swings with your arms at chest height while rotating your hips all the way back and all the way through—180 degrees of rotation. Once you have a comfortable rhythm, make a "rip" swing every second or third swing.

Short Description Baseball Rip Swing:

The second balance drill is the Baseball Rip Swing. Stand upright with your spine straight up and down (don't lean forward or take a golf stance). Hold your club chest-high, parallel to the ground, and straight out in front of you with your arms fully extended. Swing back and forth in a rhythm. Your goal is to get your belt buckle to rotate all the way to the target on your forward swing, then 180 degrees away from your target on the back swing. Work your feet so that you are pointing alternate toes at the ground at the end of the swing. Once you establish a rhythm, take a "rip" swing every 2 or 3 swings, always staying in balance (a rip swing means swing as fast as you can). Listen for the "whoosh" sound and move the whoosh as far in front of you as possible. Learn to swing as fast as you can.

Detailed Description Baseball Rip Swing

This drill is deceptively simple. You are simply making a series of continuous back and forth baseball swings chest high while rotating your hips all the way back and all the way forward through 180 degrees of rotation. Yet most of my students are significantly out of balance by the 3rd swing. What is more, most students have never even tried to see how fast they can swing, so the rip swing can easily throw them off balance.

Step 1 Baseball Rip Swing Stand Upright

Start this drill by taking a normal width to slightly wider than normal stance. Stand so your spine is completely upright and vertical. Do not lean forward or take a golf stance. You are making a baseball swing, not a golf swing. Plus, you are going to be swinging as fast as you can, so you want to hold your back and your spine in as neutral a position as possible to avoid injury. If this drill gives you any discomfort, discontinue it immediately (Note: if any of the drills give you discomfort, discontinue them immediately).

Swing Chest High

Hold your club (I usually use a driver) chest-high, parallel to the ground, and straight out in front of you with your arms fully extended. Your weight should be centered over the middle of your feet and you should be athletically balanced.

Begin swinging back and forth around your spine in a continuous rhythm. Your arms will fold appropriately as you swing back, and then they should fully extend just past the point where you would make contact with the ball if you were in a golf position. On your follow through your arms will fold and wrap around your body.

Turn Your Belt Buckle 180 Degrees

As you swing your goal is to get your belt buckle to turn backward 90 degrees away from your address position backward and then forward past your address position. This means that as you swing your belt buckle will turn completely through 180 degrees of rotation.

This is far more rotation than you will be aiming for in your regular driver swing, so again this is not intended to be your new move. But we are going to be looking for more hip turn than you are probably used to doing now, and the signal you are sending to your body is that it is good to turn the hips, particularly on the backswing.

Point Your Toes

To practice this drill effectively your feet should roll up so your left toe is pointed to the ground on the backswing, and then your right toe will end up pointed at the ground on the forward swing. The foot pointing to the ground will have virtually no weight on it. The sole of your left shoe should be completely facing the target (on the backswing), and the shoelaces of your right shoe should be completely facing the target on your follow through. You might also try thinking of first swinging right handed then swinging left handed to help you make the turn back.

Most students have no problem with pointing the right toe to the ground on the forward swing. But nearly all students initially have trouble making the complete turn to the back and pointing the left toe to the ground with no weight on the left foot.

The first couple of times you try this drill take a look at your left foot on your backswing. Very few students are able to get their foot completely turned so the sole of the shoe is facing the target. Most students only get half way, and their belt buckle doesn't turn completely away from the target. Their left foot will be turned half to three quarters of the way to the top, and there will still be weight on the left foot. The backswing is where you need to work the hardest to get all the way around, so pay the most attention to your left foot on the backswing and make sure it is turning all the way up.

Release Left Leg Tension

One of the main reasons students have such difficulty with the turn back is that they typically retain more tension in their left leg than they realize. This drill requires that you let go of all the tension in your left leg as you make your backswing.

Pay attention to your left leg as you make this swing. When you finally get the motion correct and the left toe is pointed at the ground, you will probably find that you had to let go of some muscle tension in your left leg. More than likely the muscle group you relaxed will be the same muscle group where you hold tension in your normal swing, particularly under competitive pressure.

I find that I tend to hold tension in my hamstring area. When I keep my right leg hamstring muscle relaxed my whole leg relaxes and I am able to make a tension-free swing. But everybody is different. Some students hold tension in their left quads, some in their calf muscles, some in their ankles, and some in their toes.

I encourage you to experiment with your awareness as you perform this drill so that you can find your tension spot. What muscle group do you relax to make the baseball swing?

Side Note—Release Left Leg Tension When You Are Under Pressure

An interesting side note is that when we get under pressure this tension spot in the leg tends to tighten even more without our being aware of it. This extra tension prevents a fluid, athletic swing because it inadvertently restricts your backswing. We often attribute a poor drive to a mechanical issue when the real cause was a little bit of extra tension in the left leg.

The next time you are playing and you are in a pressure situation, focus on this tension area in your left leg just prior to swinging. Relax that tension spot and then make your swing. You may be pleasantly surprised with the results.

Swing In Balance

Once you are able to make a complete, 180 degree rotation, with the toes alternately pointing to the ground and the belt buckle turned completely away from the target and then completely toward the target, focus on your balance. You should be making these swings in a continuous motion back and forth without having to take extra steps or without having to stop and reset your balance every few swings.

Your weight should be centered over your feet as you swing. Here again if you have any difficulty maintaining your balance with this drill, it is probably symptomatic of a similar balance issue in your normal swing. Pay attention to what is pulling you off balance, and where it occurs in the swing. Keep your hands relatively light on the club (grip pressure around 3 or 4 on a scale of 10) and teach yourself to swing in balance.

Rip It!

Once you can make this baseball swing with an easy, rhythmic back and forth motion and still remain in good balance, it is time to add speed. This is the "Rip it" part of "grip it and rip it."

Once you have established a few rhythmic swings, add a "rip" swing every second or third swing. Swing as fast as you can. Stay in balance. You want to hear your club "whoosh" as it zings through the air. This is your speed training. Have some fun and let it loose!

Once you have made your rip swing, fall back into your easy rhythmic swings for a couple of swings, then rip it again. Keep repeating this sequence. Try to move the whoosh sound as far out in front of you toward the target as possible when you make your rip swing. Again, the key is to stay in balance.

The Rip Sequence

Several interesting things happen when you make your rip swing, and I have seen it happen very consistently with students. As students make their backswing and get ready for their rip swing, they almost invariably start their forward swing by planting their left heel first and then initiating a weight shift to the left side while rotating their hips. Their arms naturally stay back in a lag position. The hip rotation carries the shoulders around, and the shoulders carry the club into position with lag. The club releases naturally and with significantly more speed through the impact zone.

This sequence, in this order, is exactly what you want to achieve in your full downswing.

What is interesting is that so many students follow this sequence naturally when they do this drill, yet they do exactly the opposite when hitting a golf ball. They initiate the downswing with the club, which swings the arms, which swings the shoulders, which may or may not result in a hip turn and weight shift.

You want your body to swing the club, not the club to swing your body.

Pay attention to the sequential motion and the order in which your body parts complete the swing as you make your rip swing: First the feet and legs, then the weight shift and hip turn, then the core, then the shoulders, then the arms, and finally the club. Feel your feet plant first. Feel your hips turn toward the target as you make your weight shift. Notice how this motion carries your shoulders and thus the club into position. Pay attention to the way you can generate significant swing speed even with relaxed hands and arms as long as your core is doing all the work.

Adding More Training Elements To The Baseball Rip Swing

As you are making the baseball rip swings you can add a few elements when you are comfortable. Add these elements only after you have mastered the basic drill.

Variation 1 Baseball Rip Swing: Straight Left Arm

When you make the backswing component of the rip swing, focus on keeping your left arm straight throughout the backswing and much of the forward swing. Allow your wrists to hinge at the top and the club to swing around behind you on the backswing. As you make your forward swing, keep your left arm straight and your left elbow locked until after the club has passed the impact position, when your left arm should bend and fold around your body naturally.

Keeping your left arm straight on the backswing is a good habit. It also forces your shoulders to make a more complete rotation. If you keep your left arm straight while practicing this drill you will develop a better feel for core rotation and having your body swing the club instead of having the club swing your body. A straight left arm also helps with clubhead extension and swing arc width, which will pay off in more clubhead speed and, therefore, distance.

Variation 2 Baseball Rip Swing: Tucked Right Arm

The next element you can add is to keep your right elbow bent and your right arm tucked against your body as long as possible. On the backswing bend your right elbow and tuck your right arm against your body as normal. When you start your forward swing motion, keep your right arm bent and tucked against your body until you have completely turned to face the target. In other words, keep the club back and keep your right arm from straightening out as long as possible. Then release the club. This variation can help significantly with learning how to hold lag and moving the whoosh farther forward in the swing.

I will often advise students to learn how to make this motion by resting their club on their shoulder at the top of the backswing (both your arms will need to bend to do this drill variation). Then, as the student makes their forward swing, they keep the club attached to the shoulder until their body has turned completely toward the target. The club should remain in the exact same spot on the shoulder. Only after they have completed their turn should they then release the club and swing out toward the target. This tuck position promotes a very late release, and gives you the feeling of having your body complete its turn before the clubhead releases.

You can't do this drill with a straight left arm, so don't worry about that part. The exercise here is to hold the clubhead release for as long as possible to get the sensation of holding lag and a late release. This drill really reinforces the concept of timing as well.

Variation 3 Baseball Rip Swing: "Whoosh" Swing

The next element you can add to the Baseball Rip swing is the "Whoosh" drill.

Flip your driver around so you are holding the shaft just above the clubhead. Take your normal grip on the shaft and make the same Baseball Rip swing. Because the grip end is so much lighter you will be able to generate significantly more speed than when you are swinging the clubhead, and the shaft should make a "whoosh" sound.

Pay attention to where the "whoosh" begins. You want the club to whoosh out in front of you body, toward the target. If the whoosh is behind you then you are casting or releasing early. If the whoosh is in the impact area in front of you then you are releasing too early—more than likely because you are stopping your hip rotation at impact. Learn to swing so that the whoosh happens in front of you.

This drill variation is great self-training for holding lag longer because your body will naturally figure out how to hold the club back if you are concentrating on moving the whoosh to the front.

Side Note—Practice The Baseball Rip Swing Anywhere

You can practice the Baseball Rip drill at the golf course, on the range, or at home. If you practice this drill for just 2 to 4 minutes every day for a week you will begin to see a marked improvement in your swing speed.

This is also another of those drills that I use when I get to the course to play and there is no warm up facility or no time to hit practice balls. I have found that just a few minutes of the Baseball Rip drill is as effective as 20 minutes of hitting balls on the range.

Select "Balance" on the main menu on the accompanying DVD to view the video of the Baseball Rip Swing drill. Or you can find the drill online at: http://www.targetcenteredgolf.com/videos/baseball_rip_swing.html

Balance Drill #3: Toe Tap

Purpose

Balance and weight shift check at the Finish Position.

Swing Thought

Tap, tap, tap, pick up (the foot)

Short Description Toe Tap

The third balance drill is the Toe Tap Drill. Make your normal swing and hit a ball. When you finish your swing, your right foot should be pointed to the ground. Finish the rotation of your swing and tap your right toe against the ground three times, then pick up your right foot. Stay in balance without wobbling, tilting, or falling over.

Detailed Description Toe Tap

This is another drill that is deceptively simple. A surprising number of students have difficulty at first with this drill. It is also one of the first drills I use with juniors, particularly boys who play a lot of baseball.

To get maximum distance you need to transfer as much momentum as possible through the ball toward the target. If you are leaving weight on your right foot at impact or even on the finish, you are not efficiently using momentum and you have a power leak.

The Drill

Make a full swing, hit a ball, tap your right toe on the ground three times and then hold up your right foot off the ground. With more practice you'll learn to avoid wobbling, leaning or falling over. The objective is to completely finish your swing with all your weight on your left foot and your hips facing toward the target.

What To Look For

Your weight should be to the outside of your left foot, in most cases with the left foot slightly rolled over so the weight is actually on the outside edge of the left foot. You should feel as though your weight is centered straight down your body line through your left ankle, into the ground (much like you experienced with the tight ankles drill). There is normally a slight delay after impact while your body completes its rotation before you can comfortably tap your back foot.

This drill combines a focus on weight shift with balance—two key elements of all golf swings. Your swing thought should be simply "tap, tap, tap" and hold up your foot.

Benefits Of The Toe Tap Drill

Mastering this drill is very important for achieving a complete release as well as learning how to extend to the target. If you cannot master this drill you may face some physiological challenges that will prevent you from achieving maximum swing speed through the ball.

For instance, if you are unable to get your weight completely to your left side and if you cannot turn your hips to the target, your body will place a physiological constraint on how far you can extend your arms toward the target before you either cup your wrist or chicken wing your left arm. If you have a chicken wing action in your swing and have access to a video, watch your hip rotation during the swing. If your hips stop rotating while your arms go through the impact zone it is almost impossible to avoid having the left elbow bend—the chicken wing.

If you can get your weight to your left side and your hips to the target you can achieve full extension. If you can maintain hip rotation during the swing your chicken wing will tend to go away by itself.

Physiological Constraints

Try this simple experiment. Take a golf stance without a club and extend your arms down to their normal address position. Put your palms together and keep your arms straight. Without moving your hips, attempt to swing your arms to the left toward the target. With straight arms most students are barely able to extend their hands past their left thigh. To go farther in the swing they must allow their left arm to break down and chicken wing.

Now do the same experiment, but instead of moving your arms while your hips are locked into position, keep your hands locked in a position straight out in front of you. Then move your hips to the target, allowing your arms to come along for the ride. Keeping your left arm straight and achieving extension toward the target should be easy and comfortable, as long as the hips rotate toward the target at the same time as the arms.

In the first case your body simply won't allow your arms to swing out any farther toward the target. You have a physiological constraint.

When I work with students who have a chicken wing issue and I show them a video of their swing, we often see that their hips stop rotating through the impact zone. Momentum keeps the arms swinging through, but the body prevents the arms from extending out because the hips have stopped moving. With no place left to go the left arm has to break down or the hands have to flip and the left wrist will cup. The chicken wing or the wrist cup is not the problem. It is actually the symptom of a larger issue—not enough hip rotation to the target.

We'll talk more about this issue when we examine hip rotation. But for purposes of this drill the lesson is to get the weight to the left side while staying in balance. Quite often the result of a more balanced weight shift is to facilitate a more constant hip turn.

Adding More Training Elements To The Toe Tap Drill

Variation 1: Hold Your Finish

Holding your finish is less an extension of the Toe Tap drill than a good habit to form for all your golf swings.

When you complete your normal golf shot, hold your finish position until the ball hits the ground. This means holding your finish for 3 to 5 seconds after impact.

There are two good reasons to develop this good habit. First, I saw Tiger Woods give this advice to a junior golfer during a clinic. If the world's best golfer believes it is a good idea to hold your finish then it makes sense to take his advice.

Second, holding your finish will reveal your true balance position. Like the Toe Tap drill, if you are out of balance at the finish of your golf swing, holding your finish until the ball hits the ground will usually reveal where your weight really is at the finish and how well you got through the swing.

I recommend you use this technique on all your golf swings, including your practice shots. This habit takes very little effort to put into place and it will tell you much about your swings.

The other benefit you will gain from holding your finish will be your increased ability to complete an effective post-shot routine and analysis. Later in the book I have included a section on conducting a post-shot routine. Holding your finish is an integral element of that routine.

Select "Balance" on the main menu of the accompanying DVD to view the video of the Toe Tap drill. Or you can find the drill online at: http://www.targetcenteredgolf.com/videos/toe_tap.html

6

DISTANCE KEY #2: LEVERAGE

This part of the instruction deals with a fundamental position of the powerful golf swing. What you will learn here will be true whether you want to hit the ball long or with consistency. It involves a concept I refer to as "leverage."

What do I mean by leverage?

Think of a moment when you might have been pushing something heavy. Imagine yourself pushing a car that has stalled or is stuck in a rut. If you were to stand sideways to the car and put your left shoulder to the bumper to get ready to push, you would dig your right foot in to get a really good purchase. When you begin to push, you will push from the inside of your right foot—from the ball of your foot—and drive your legs.

The Ball Of Your Right Foot

Your foot—and more specifically the inside part of the ball of your right foot where your arch meets the ball of your foot—represents your leverage point. If you lose your leverage—if your foot slips—you lose the power you were applying to the push.

Now imagine trying to push that same car from the same position, but instead of putting your weight on the inside part of your right foot, you put your weight on the outside part of your right foot. Would you be able to apply the same force to the push? Of course not. You might not be able to push at all. In fact, if your weight is far enough outside your right foot you would find that any push you applied to the car would more than likely propel you away from the car.

In the golf swing the concept is much the same.

Your Leverage Point

The inside part of the ball of your right foot is your leverage point.

If you allow your weight to drift over the top of your foot or even to the outside edge of your foot, you lose your leverage. You will have nothing to push with to initiate the downswing.

If your weight is flat over your right foot or on the outside of it, you will either slide your hips back to the inside to re-establish your leverage point, or you will start your downswing with your upper body. Neither the hip slide nor starting the swing with the upper body produces swing speed. In fact, they are usually significant power leaks.

Your Leverage Point Is The Key To Power And Consistency

Maintaining your leverage position at the top of your backswing is one of the most important keys to both distance and consistency. In fact, you could consider that the whole purpose of the backswing to be nothing more than an opportunity to load as much power as possible on the inside part of the ball of your right foot.

Your timing, your pivot, and your core speed are all directly dependent on your leverage position.

When I first started working to increase my swing speed I was not consistent with my leverage point. On video I could see that my head was moving backward at impact. But I didn't know the cause.

The more I studied swing speed the more I realized that I had to transfer as much momentum as possible through the ball at the point of impact. The fact that my head was moving backward at impact meant that I was leaking momentum and therefore power.

Transfer Momentum **Through** The Ball

I was fortunate to get some solid swing advice from my coach, Ernie Barbour, who helped me to understand the root cause of my backward momentum.

In essence, the advice I received was to keep my hips relatively level throughout the swing, rather than have my left hip point down toward the ball on the backswing. Ernie described it as stacking my hip bones over the top of my right knee at the top. I got the concept right away, and within a couple of swings I was able to make a different swing with a flatter hip angle, or what we referred to as a flat belt angle throughout the swing.

With just a couple of rounds of practice it all came together for me, and my swing speed took a major leap. I went a step beyond Ernie's analysis and put together the leverage concept that propelled me to a world championship.

Set Your Leverage Point At Address

My normal address position has my knees slightly bent inward— knock-kneed, as opposed to bow-legged. In this position my right knee is an inch or two inside the ball of my right foot. I squeeze my knees slightly together (not enough to create unwanted tension, particularly in the left leg, but enough to set the legs in position to react naturally during my swing). This slight squeeze predisposes both legs to move in the correct direction during the swing.

As I take my backswing my right knee naturally rotates as my hips turn. Everybody's swing does much the same thing.

What I had not realized before I put together the leverage concept that propelled me to the world long drive title, was that I was actually over-rotating on my right knee and allowing my weight to drift over the top of my right foot. It is a relatively comfortable position to have your weight flat on top of your foot. It feels stable. However, it is not a position of stored power waiting to be released.

This poor position I now refer to as flat-footed.

The Flat-Footed Swing Power Loss

The excess downward left hip tilt I was using prior to my discovery was causing my right knee to stack flat on top of my right foot (instead of the ball of my foot), and further causing my right hip to stack on top of my right knee. But my center of mass was still inside my right foot. In essence I had a split leverage axis—one half of the axis was running straight up from my flat foot through my knee to my hip, and another axis began at my hip and angled into the middle of my body, toward my center of mass.

Imagine trying to use a lever with a hinge in the middle. You could strain away with all your might moving the top part of the lever, but no matter how much you tried, the bottom part of the lever would not move. You won't have very much power at the bottom of the lever.

The result of this split lever position was that I would throw my hips at the ball, hoping that I could catch up on the timing at impact by flipping my hands through the hitting area. Sometimes my timing would be perfect and I could generate a terrific drive. But when my timing was off it was anybody's guess where the ball would go.

In most cases when my timing was off (usually too fast), I would slide my hips forward and I would either block the ball right or hit a slice. In the worst case my hips wouldn't move at all and I would start my swing from the top with my hands and arms, creating an over-the-top move that caused a pull or a pull hook.

The point is that I could hit the ball either right or left, but the underlying cause was the same issue—poor leverage position. My weight was flat over the top of my right foot, not on the inside where the true leverage is located.

The picture you might draw in your mind to find the ideal leverage position at the top of your swing is to keep your right knee over the ball of your right foot. Then you rotate your hips until they feel as though they are over the top of your right knee. Then you stack your center of mass over your hips. This creates a straight line axis of power—an extremely powerful leverage position at the top of the backswing.

This leverage position leads directly to effortless power.

Leverage Gives You Effortless Power

You are making maximal use of your big muscles from a highly leveraged position, which allows you to unwind on your downswing from the ground up. When you unwind from the ground up on your downswing you create maximum torque, maximum lag, and maximum clubhead speed at impact.

Take a moment to consider again the picture of stacking your right knee over the ball of your right foot, stacking your hips over your right knee, and then stacking your center of mass over your hips. Compare that image to your current swing. This area is where I generally find the largest power leaks in student swings.

Leverage Concept: The Power "X"

I'm going to take a moment here to explain the relationship between power and tension, and how the two should work in harmony to create swing speed. Since we are discussing power and leverage here I want to make sure you are clear on what muscles you should use to store and deliver power effectively. This concept has been extremely helpful for most of my students. I think it is worth your consideration.

The concept is called the Power-X.

The idea is that you have one axis composed of your left arm and right leg that are dynamically powerful and active during the swing.

You have another axis composed of your right arm and left leg that should be tension-free during the swing.

Imagine standing upright and crossing your arms straight down in front of you across your mid-section so your right arm points down to your left leg and your left arm points down toward your right leg. Your arms make an "X" across your core mid-section. One axis—your left arm/right leg—is your power axis. The other axis is your tension-free axis.

Protagonistic Vs. Antagonistic Muscles In The Power-X

To understand how your muscles either work in harmony or against each other to achieve swing speed, imagine doing some weight lifting and performing a curl with your arms. When you raise the weight your biceps are activated. The biceps contract to lift the weight and relax to lower the weight to perform the curl. They are dynamically strong and active throughout the exercise.

The muscles you use to lift the weight—primarily your biceps—are your protagonist muscles. They do all the work.

While you are doing this exercise your triceps muscles are relatively inactive. If you were to tense up your triceps during this exercise it would suddenly become very difficult to raise the weight.

Your triceps muscles are your antagonistic muscles. They do not assist in raising or lowering the weight, and when they are tense they make it very difficult for the biceps to do their job.

The Power-X works much the same way. (Note: this is not the X-Factor, which I cover later).

Left Arm/Right Leg Power Axis

During the swing the left arm and right leg are your protagonistic muscles. They are strong and powerful and in control of the swing. They do all the work. All the muscles on the left arm/right leg axis do the facilitative work of generating clubhead speed. I call this your Power Axis.

In contrast, all the muscles on the right arm/left leg axis are the antagonistic muscles. They should feel as though they are along for the ride. If the muscles in this antagonistic axis have tension, they will work against generating clubhead speed. These muscles need to be tension-free, thus I call this axis the Tension-Free Axis.

This concept came about as I was attempting to help a student relax and take a tension-free swing. This student was very right-side dominant in his swing and his grip pressure was so strong it was off the charts. Each time I asked the student to relax prior to swinging he would relax all the muscles in his body. Both his arms would drop as he let go of tension. I was attempting to get him to relax his right arm tension, but instead all the muscles in both arms would go limp.

I came up with the Power-X concept to help him understand the dynamic power needs of the swing. When you are practicing your leverage drills, and indeed all you drills, keep the Power-X concept in mind. Keep the left arm and right leg strong and powerful, and keep the right arm and left leg tension free. You will quickly be making more effortless swings.

Leverage Drills

The drills outlined below are all designed to help you understand how to achieve a straight-line axis of power with a leveraged position at the top of your backswing. Click on the link to see the video drills.

Select "Leverage" on the main menu of the accompanying DVD to view these Leverage drills. You can find the drills online at http://www.targetcenteredgolf.com/videos/slant_board.html

Leverage Drill #1: Slant Board
Leverage Drill #2: Right Knee Set
Leverage Drill #3: Toe Press & Tee Drop

Just as you saw with the Balance drills, each Leverage drill below will have a Purpose, Swing Thought, Short Description, and Long Description, as well as Variations and Additional Training Elements. Again, master the leverage position only after you have mastered your dynamic balance (balance in motion throughout the swing). After some practice with these leverage drills, your effortless power will come from your leverage position as you learn to make the best use of your large muscles and your core body rotation.

Leverage Drill #1: Slant Board

Purpose

Keep your weight on the inside part of the ball of your right foot and maintain your leverage position at the top of the swing

Swing Thought

Weight Inside

Use the butt-end of a shaft along the outside edge of your right foot to provide an angle and brace to help keep your weight on the inside part of your right foot at the top of the backswing. Use the bracing effect of the shaft to push off during the downswing to add power at impact.

Short Description Slant Board

The slant board drill uses the butt end of a shaft along the outside part of the right foot to angle the right foot in. Use the angle produced by the slant board under your right foot to help keep your weight on the inside part of your right foot throughout the backswing—and particularly at the top of the backswing. Start the down swing by pushing off the slant board to drive the hips through the pivot. Finish the swing with your weight on the left side and your right toe pointed to the ground. Keep your focus on where your weight is at the top of the backswing to develop an awareness of how your weight shifts during the swing, and learn how to make a weight shift without losing your leverage position.

Long Description Slant Board Drill

The concept behind the slant board drill is to use an outside device to put your foot at such an angle that it is difficult to be in any other position other than the correct leverage position throughout the swing. At the top of your swing your weight should be centered over the inside part of the ball of your right foot in an athletic, powerful position that will allow you to drive toward the target with your legs and hips on the downswing.

Step 1 Slant Board: Normal Stance

Start this drill by addressing the ball in your normal stance position. Have on hand (down by your right foot) something you can place under the outside edge of your right foot.

I like to use the grip end of an old shaft. It's not a board, per se (even though we call this a slant board drill), but it will accomplish the same end. An old shaft grip is about an inch high, which is about all you need to produce the right amount of slant on the right foot to accomplish this drill but still have the swing feel like a normal swing. You could use a 1x6 board or a piece of pvc pipe just as easily.

The key is to have something about an inch high that can support the entire length of your foot. I don't recommend using a golf ball for this drill because it is too high and does not support your entire foot in a stable position.

Step 2 Slant Board: Insert A Prop Under Your Right Foot

Once you are at your normal address position tilt your right foot in and slide the old grip under the outside edge of your entire right foot. Be sure to get the grip under your heel and the wide part of your foot so your entire foot is supported. Your foot will slant in toward the center of your stance, and your right knee will also likely move slightly farther inward than your normal stance.

From this starting position it is easier to keep your weight on the inside part of the ball of your right foot throughout your backswing and particularly at the top of the backswing.

Step 3 Slant Board: Focus On Your Leverage Position

Make your normal swing and focus on how the slant board keeps your right foot in a leverage position throughout the backswing. Because the slant board is only an inch high this drill should be similar enough to your regular swing that it should not cause any unusual swing changes other than to keep your weight centered over the correct leverage spot. You should be able to make your normal weight shift and pivot.

Your goal with this drill is to learn what it feels like to make a weight shift during the backswing while keeping your weight over your leverage point—the inside part of the right foot—during an otherwise normal golf swing.

Note: Support Position Caution

When you practice this drill, be sure the grip/prop on the ground is on the **outside** part of your right foot. Do not put the old grip under the middle of your foot or you may run the risk of rolling your right foot over the top of the grip and injuring your ankle.

Note: Finish The Swing

Also, it is quite common for students who are using this drill for the first time to finish their swing and leave their right foot still attached to the grip, as though their foot is glued to the grip. Students become so focused on getting their weight on the inside of their right foot and keeping it there that they forget to transfer their weight to their left side on the finish.

Allow your right foot to come off the shaft the same way you would in a normal golf swing, finishing with the right toe pointed to the ground and your weight on your left side.

Push Off Like Runner's Blocks

In fact, it has been helpful for some students to think of the grip as a device put in place specifically to help them push off, much the same way sprinters use runner's blocks to get a powerful start to their race.

Remember that the purpose of this drill is to help you maintain your leverage position throughout the backswing. Remember, too, that the purpose of the backswing is to load power into the right leg so that you can drive toward the target on the downswing. The image of a sprinter at the starting line loading power into his legs and then driving off the runner's blocks may help you facilitate the correct driving action that starts the downswing from a leveraged top-of-backswing position.

Adding More Training Elements To The Slant Board Drill

Squeeze the Knees

An additional element that can be added to the Slant Board drill is to squeeze your knees together lightly before initiating the backswing. When you are in your normal address position, take your range bucket (or something about the size of a volleyball. I sometimes use balloons with students as well) and place it between your knees so your knees and inner thighs gently squeeze the bucket.

Remove the bucket but keep your knees in the new, inward-canted address position. Swing away and let your legs work naturally. Many students see an immediate improvement in their lower body movement with this simple set-up adjustment.

Squeezing the knees together, or setting up slightly "knock-kneed" prior to the swing, has several advantages. The main advantage is that it predisposes the legs to work correctly.

The right knee is canted inward, pre-setting the leverage position on the inside part of the right foot and providing a stable base for the pivot. On the backswing, you turn against the right leg.

The left knee is also canted inward, predisposing it to fold inward toward the ball on the backswing. With a gentle squeeze on the bucket prop you can maintain low tension in the left leg at address and allow the leg to move backward on the backswing. The backward (and slightly inward) motion of the left leg facilitates a good hip turn, which in turn leads to more distance off the tee.

Select "Leverage" on the main menu of the accompanying DVD to view the Slant Board drill. Or you can find the drill online at: http://www.targetcenteredgolf.com/videos/slant_board.html

Leverage Drill #2: Right Knee Set

Purpose

Focus on keeping the same flex and relative position of the right knee throughout the backswing and the start of the downswing.

Swing Thought

Knee in.

Short Description Right Knee Set

The second leverage drill focuses on setting the right knee at the appropriate athletic flex, and then maintaining that flex and knee position throughout the backswing. The right knee should be slightly flexed and located inside of your foot line, such that if you drew a straight line down from the outside edge of your right kneecap to the ground, the line should hit a point on the ground just inside the ball of your right foot. On the backswing the knee will rotate as the rest of your core rotates, but the relative position will remain inside the vertical line represented by the ball of your right foot. Think of the area from your foot to your knee as a post driven into the ground. Your entire swing will rotate around this post on the backswing. Work also to keep the same relative knee flex level during the backswing. Do not straighten up your right leg on the backswing (a common power leak), and do not squat either. Keep the right knee in the same position and flex through the top of the backswing. "Set" the right knee at address, and then maintain that set position. Your swing thought is "knee in" throughout the entire swing.

Detailed Description Right Knee Set

The second leverage drill focuses on setting the right knee at address in an athletic position and then maintaining that set position during the backswing. Maintaining your right knee set will help with both consistency and power for all swings.

If you currently change your right knee flex during the backswing you will require a compensating movement at some time during the downswing. Very commonly you may slide your hips toward the target in an attempt to regain your leverage position. Alternatively, you may squat on the downswing, or you may leave your weight on your right foot through impact.

Any time you stand up during the backswing you change your spine angle. Getting back to your square address position requires perfect timing. It can be done, but if your timing is off you will have difficulty generating power or striking the ball on the center of the clubface.

Step 1: "Set" The Right Knee At Address

To practice the Right Knee Set drill, take your normal stance and address position. Focus on your right knee. Prior to starting your swing, imagine your right knee as "set" in space. The knee can rotate, but it should not slide to the right and it should not straighten up. It may be helpful just prior to starting the backswing to put a little extra force on the inside part of the right foot before making the swing to keep the knee anchored. You may also try turning the knee in slightly just before swinging. Be careful not to open up the hips if you do.

Step 2: Focus On The Knee During The Swing

Make an otherwise normal golf swing but keep your attention on your right knee, particularly during the backswing. Pay attention to any lateral movement of the knee that would cause your weight to shift over the top or outside part of your right foot. Your knee should be free to rotate, but it shouldn't slide to the right. Also note any tendency of the right knee to straighten up or to otherwise change from the original flex position set at address.

Allow your right knee (and your right side) to drive through the ball as normal on the downswing. Finish with your weight on the left side, with the hips facing the target and the right toe pointed into the ground.

Knee Set Variation 1: Shaft Drill

You can attempt to do this Right Knee Set drill on your own or you can use a training aid. One additional way I use the old shaft is to stick the narrow end in the ground about 8 inches in front of my right toe and then angle the shaft so that it is braced against the outside of my right knee at address (this is for a grass hitting surface). The grip end of the old shaft will extend in back of my right knee and out of play.

During my swing I pay attention to the feel of the old shaft against the outside part of my right knee. I make a normal swing, keeping the pressure against the shaft as light as possible, and not moving the shaft. The angle of the shaft should provide clearance for your right foot so you can finish your swing in a normal position.

The shaft against your knee provides kinesthetic feedback to help you feel the action in your right knee. You can pay attention to the feel of the shaft during the swing while still keeping your eye on the ball to make solid contact.

Knee Set Variation 2: Pigeon-Toe Drill

An alternative way to feel the leverage position during your backswing is to practice the "pigeon toe" drill. In this variation you take your normal stance and address. Before you start your backswing, slide your right heel out to the right so just your right foot is turned in toward the ball—in other words, in a pigeon toe position. Your left foot stays in its original, normal position.

"Set" your right knee position and flex. Once you set your right knee, maintain the set position through the backswing.

Check your hip alignment once your right heel has been pushed out to be sure you square your hips back up. It is quite common when turning the right foot inward to have the hips open up left. This drill should be done from as square a posture as possible.

Make a ¾ swing and pay attention to the added torque in your right leg during the swing. Keep your right leg at the same flex and position.

Most students are immediately aware of increased tension in their right leg all the way up through their right hip. They also experience an immediate sense of "driving" through the ball. Be careful during this drill not to over swing and cause too much tension in the right leg and knee so as to cause injury.

To a large extent the torque position you feel during the pigeon toe drill is nearly the way your normal driver position should feel at the top. You should strive for this position and feeling of power in the right leg for all your drives.

Knee Set Variation 3: Bucket Drills

Side Bucket Position

Another variation of the Knee Set drill is to use an alternative training aid found at nearly all driving ranges—your range bucket.

Take your normal stance and address position. Before starting your backswing, put your range bucket up against your right leg on the outside part of your right foot near the ankle and heel. Squeeze your knees together slightly. Most range buckets have an angle that quite nicely matches the angle of your lower leg at address. The bucket should fit snugly up against your leg.

As you make your swing, pay attention to the feel of the bucket against your lower leg. You should not move or otherwise tip the bucket on your backswing. Your right knee will rotate, but you should still be able to make a weight shift into the right leg without tipping the bucket.

Back Bucket Position

The second place to put the range bucket is directly behind your right heel at address to enhance your awareness of whether your right leg is straightening.

The flex in your right leg at address should allow the angle of the bucket to nearly match the angle of your leg, so you should be able to snug the bucket right up against your heel and calf muscle. Pay attention to the feel of the bucket against the back of your calf and make your swing without moving or tipping the bucket on the backswing. Sometimes your heel action will knock the bucket over after impact. That is ok.

Pay Attention To Maintaining The Same Flex

The point of this knee set/bucket variation is to help you feel any straightening or sliding of your right leg on the backswing. If you straighten your right leg you have a power leak, even if you maintain your leverage. You will not have stored any power in your leg muscles that could be used to drive your hips and core through the ball to the target. You may have great leverage, but you will have lost your athleticism, and your body will attempt to compensate by sliding on the downswing or producing an arm swing.

Select "Leverage" on the main menu of the accompanying DVD to view the Right Knee Set drill. Or you can find the drill online at: http://www.targetcenteredgolf.com/videos/right_knee_set.html

Leverage Drill #3: Right Toe Press and Tee Drop

Purpose

Focus on keeping the weight forward and inside the ball of the right foot at the top of the backswing.

This picture sequence shows the tee being placed under the ball of the right foot. If just the tip of the tee is placed under the edge of the shoe the tee will pop up when pressure is applied.

The object of the drill is to keep the tee in the air all the way through impact.

The third picture shows what happens to the tee when weight is transferred to the outside of the right foot during the backswing. The tee drops (you want to avoid letting the tee drop).

Swing Thought

Press down your big toe.

Short Description Toe Press & Tee Drop

The third leverage drill uses a tee placed under the big toe or the ball of your foot. If you place the pointed end of the tee just under the ball of your right foot and press down, the tee should stick up. During the swing, keep pressure on your big toe and the ball of your right foot to keep the tee in the air. Have a friend watch the tee. If the tee drops, you are losing your leverage position. The tee won't interfere with your normal finish, so make sure you complete your swing with your hips to the target and the right toe pointed into the ground. Your swing thought is "press down with your big toe" during the entire swing until just after impact when you release the pressure to finish your swing.

Long Description Toe Press & Tee Drop

The third leverage drill involves keeping force or leverage on the inside part of your right foot at the top of the swing.

Try this drill first by pressing down with your big toe during the backswing. Press your toe flat down against the inside your shoe (rather than curling your toes to grab). The act of pressing down with your big toe will keep the force of your swing in the forward part of your foot and help you to maintain your leverage position.

Keep pressing down with the big toe all the way through impact, and then release the pressure after you hit the ball to finish your swing. Your swing thought during this drill is "press down with your big toe."

This drill has been very helpful for students who have a tendency to allow their weight to drift to the outside part of their right foot at the top, and for those who allow their weight to shift back to their right heel.

Variation 1: Tee Drop

This variation of the Toe Press drill uses a tee as a marker to see how effective you are at maintaining your leverage position. It is best to have a friend or observer who can tell you what happens to the tee during the swing, because you will not be able to see the tee move as you are hitting.

Place the narrow end of a tee under your right toe or under the ball of your right foot. If you place just the tip of the tee underneath the edge of your shoe and press down, the tee should lift up. The goal is to keep the tee in its lifted position throughout the swing, and particularly at the top of the backswing. You should be able to maintain consistent pressure on the tee throughout the swing, until you release after impact and roll up on top of the tee.

Select "Leverage" on the main menu of the accompanying DVD to view the Toe Press drill. Or you can find the drill online at: http://www.targetcenteredgolf.com/videos/toe_press.html

7

DISTANCE KEY #3: ARC WIDTH

The third key to getting more distance is developing a wide swing arc.

Consider the laws of physics. Imagine an old-fashioned record or a CD. As it spins, the outside of the disc will spin much faster than the inside. The farther you get from the spindle, or the axis of rotation, the faster the speed of the outside edge.

The same concept holds true with the golf club. The farther the clubhead is from the axis of rotation—in this case your spine—the faster it will travel.

The idea is that you want to create the widest possible swing arc but still keep the swing under control—meaning wide, but not at the expense of your balance or your leverage position.

There are several elements of fundamentally sound golf swings that will facilitate a wider swing arc. The first is to quiet your hands on

71

the backswing. The second is to start with a straight left arm and left elbow and then to keep the elbow straight throughout the backswing and impact. The third element is to allow your upper body to move to the right two or three inches to facilitate your weight shift, pivot, and extension.

Quiet Hands On The Takeaway

The first element of creating a wider swing arc is to quiet the hands on the takeaway. As a rule of thumb (something I have seen consistently with virtually all my students) the longer you can delay hinging your wrists on the backswing the longer you will be able to retain lag in your downswing.

The best takeaway involves keeping the hands neutral during the takeaway and not hinging the wrists until your hands are above your belt line. Far too many students take the club away with an immediate hinge, or with a grabbing or snatching motion with their hands. This results in an early hinge. The grabbing action also results in unwanted extra grip pressure, which negatively affects timing as well as your ability to hold lag. This invariably causes a cast from the top or an early release of lag during the downswing.

Early Hinge Means Early Release

I have seen a very consistent relationship in my own swing and among students regarding timing of the hinge. The earlier students hinge in the backswing, the earlier they unhinge in the downswing. Since you are attempting to maintain lag as long as possible in order to increase clubhead speed through impact, a delayed hinge on the backswing will help to promote a later release of lag.

Consistent Grip Pressure

Once you set your grip pressure before the takeaway there should be no additional grip pressure change during the initiation of the backswing. A normal grip pressure is between 4 and 6 on a scale of 10 for the driver. Any grip pressure above a 6 will cause excess tension in your arm and shoulder muscles and will actually slow down your swing speed.

When I am playing golf to score, my grip pressure is about a 5 for the driver (on a scale of 1 to 10). When I am in long drive competitions it actually drops to a 3, because I know that the less tension I have in my hands and arms the faster I will be able to rotate the club through impact and the longer I will be able to hold lag. The lighter grip pressure makes me somewhat less accurate, but the trade-off is worth it in terms of additional distance, which is my goal in long drive competitions.

Whatever grip pressure results in your best combination of distance and accuracy it is more important to have a consistent pressure than it is to shoot for one particular pressure level.

Varying your grip pressure during the swing results in a variety of issues at contact, none of which will work in your favor.

It will pay off in distance as well as your scoring accuracy goals to build some awareness around your grip pressure and what your hands do throughout the swing. Most students have not paid much attention to how their hands work throughout the swing. By paying attention, they suddenly realize that many of their mishit shots can be traced back to this inconsistency.

Swing Arc Width Drills

Below you will find drills designed to facilitate the development of a wider swing arc. To view all the drills select "Swing Arc" from the main menu of the accompanying DVD.

Swing Arc Drill #1: Low and Slow Drill
Swing Arc Drill #2: Tee Back Drill
Swing Arc Drill #3: Parallel Clubs Drill

As with all the other drills you will find the basic drill description as well as variations for practice. Master the basic drill first, and then add components as you need them.

Swing Arc Drill #1: Low And Slow

Purpose

One-body take-away, connected swing, pull the shoulder under the chin, wider swing arc.

Swing Thought

Low and Slow

Short Description Low And Slow Drill

The Low and Slow drill is one of those pieces of golf advice that is older than the hills, but it stands the test of time. As you take your backswing, keep the club low to the ground for the first two feet back, brushing the grass if possible. In essence, take your time to initiate the swing. You can use this drill in conjunction with the tee back drill (see the next drill) to help achieve good extension, stay on plane, and improve timing. The timing ratio of the backswing compared to the downswing is 3-to-1. That is, it takes three beats to complete your backswing and only one to complete your downswing (think of a waltz beat).

Use the first full beat to move the club only 2 feet, brushing the grass on the way back. Think Low & Slow. Your entire body should take the club back so you feel connected in a one-piece (or what I refer to as a one-body) takeaway. Keeping the club low to the ground on the takeaway will facilitate rotating the left shoulder underneath the chin, which will allow for a full turn without affecting your head position or spine angle.

Long Description Low And Slow Drill

After the advice to "keep my head down" during the swing, taking the club back "low and slow" was probably the second golf tip I ever learned. Keeping your driver low and slow to the ground as you initiate your takeaway helps with a variety of swing mechanics that all work in your favor when it comes to distance.

1. Keeping your driver low to the ground helps with swing width by starting your extension early in the swing, making it easier and more natural to continue with a wide extension throughout the rest of the swing

2. As you sweep your driver back low to the ground you will help your left shoulder rotate underneath your chin. This further aids in swing width without causing your head to rise and your spine angle to change—common problems that arise when the left shoulder moves the chin on the backswing.

3. Keeping your driver low on the takeaway helps to prevent the hands from hinging too early, which helps to maintain lag on the downswing.

4. Taking the club back slowly also helps to keep the hands neutral and avoids jerking the club back or the increased grip pressure and tension caused by grabbing or snatching the club at the start of the swing.

5. Taking the club back slowly allows the entire body to participate in the backswing for a one-body takeaway, helping you to stay connected during the entire swing.

6. Taking the club back slowly helps with timing and helps players avoid rushing the transition from backswing to downswing. This helps to avoid casting or an early release.

7. The mechanics of this drill are simple. Take your normal address position. As you initiate your backswing you should feel as though the bottom of your club brushes the top of the grass for almost two feet in back of the ball.

8. If you were to imagine a tee box with dew-covered grass, your job on the takeaway is to brush the dew off the grass for as

long you can on your backswing. I use the word "brush" with intent, because it implies a slower backswing motion. You are not trying to fling the dew off the grass or swipe it off the top.

Swing Tempo

Strike tee on backswing

Move tee back

Several people have studied the tempo and timing of PGA Professionals and there is a remarkable consistency to their swings. Regardless of how fast they swing, the pros almost always show a 3 to 1 timing ratio between the backswing and the downswing. That is, it takes 3 beats to make the backswing and 1 beat to make the downswing.

Three beats is a perfect waltz tempo, so if you are looking for a magic rhythm for your driver, find a good waltz song and mentally count "one-two-three-SWING-two-three" in your next practice session. It should take you the entire three beats to get the club to the top of your swing.

If you are performing this rhythm swinging drill and you are counting in your head but find that your club is already at the top of your backswing before you count to two, your swing might be a bit fast. Slowing down your backswing will allow your body to catch up. Fast backswings are nearly always arm swings, and the last thing you want to do is take your body out of the equation when you are swinging for distance.

Slow down your backswing and allow your body to rotate back so it can store the power it will need on the downswing. Take the full three beats to get to the top of your swing.

Variation 1 Low And Slow Drill: The Patience Drill

You need to store kinetic energy in your core muscles on the backswing in order to maximize your swing speed at impact. An additional way for you to allow your body to catch up with your arms is the "Patience" drill.

Take your normal backswing, but at the top of your swing allow your arms to come to a complete stop and for the club to set. When the hands and arms are stopped at the top, say the word "patience" and then unleash your downswing. You need only pause long enough at the top to say patience, so it is a very short pause.

Remember, though, that patience is not just a word, it is a concept, so it is a great word to use as a reminder to help with your timing. This pause is just long enough to allow your core to catch up with your arms and make maximum use of your leverage position on your downswing. Note: I typically use the patience drill and the waltz rhythm drill in sequence, one after the other, or as part of a 3 drill rotation with another rhythm or tempo drill.

Select "Swing Arc" on the main menu of the accompanying DVD to view the Low and Slow drill. Or you can find the drill online at: http://www.targetcenteredgolf.com/videos/low_and_slow.html

Swing Arc Drill #2: Tee Back Drill

Purpose

Lengthening the swing arc and widening the swing.

Swing Thought

Extend or Reach.

Short Description Tee Back Drill

The goal of the Tee Back drill is to help you maximize your swing width. Place a tee in the ground in back of the ball along the path your clubhead will be making. Start with the tee approximately 6 inches farther away from the ball than your right foot position. Place the tee on the inside line of the ball to allow for the slight inside line of your clubhead as you keep your swing on plane. Make your swing and listen for the noise of the clubhead contacting the tee on the backswing. If you miss the tee on your backswing, stop your swing without hitting the ball and start over at address. Practice until you can consistently hit the tee on each backswing. Then gradually move the tee farther back away from the ball until you can no longer hit the tee. When you move the tee so far back you can no longer hit it on the backswing, move the tee closer by a half-inch and practice until you can consistently make contact with the tee in that position. Then move the tee farther back and repeat the process.

Long Description Tee Back Drill

The essence of the Tee Back drill is simple. Place a tee in the ground along the line of your backswing (or if you are hitting off mats, place the tee upright, in back of the ball, along the line of your backswing). Make your swing and hit the tee on your backswing. If you miss the tee or don't hear the "tick" sound as you swing the club back, stop your swing and start over at address.

This was one of the first drills I practiced when I started to gear up for long drive competitions. I believed at first that a big key to distance was the width of the swing. But as I worked on my club extension away from the ball my accuracy fell off dramatically. I could make my swing arc much wider, but the effort was pulling my weight back and causing me to lose my athletic balance.

After a considerable amount of practice I realized it was critical to master balance and leverage first before it was possible to make the best use of a wider swing arc. Without good balance and without maintaining leverage throughout the swing it is very difficult to maintain consistency.

It took me a solid week of daily practice to rein in my swing so I could hit the grid. This experience helped me to focus on the elements of distance in a logical sequence. It also helped me understand that mastering certain fundamental concepts in a natural progression leads to the most significant improvement. This is why it is important to master the B.L.A.S.T. concepts in the order they are presented.

Step 1: Line Up To The Target

Pick out a target you will be hitting to with your drives. Temporarily take your address stance and note where your right foot is located. Locate a spot on the ground approximately 6 inches in back of your right foot and along the line of your intended driver swing path.

Once you identify a spot in back of the ball, stand behind that spot in line with the ball and the target. Place the tee straight back along the line from the target to the ball. Use the inside part of the ball to line up (as you are looking at the target from behind this would be the left side of the ball) to account for the slight inward arc of the driver head on the backswing.

Step 2: Hit The Tee On The Backswing

On your backswing you should be able to hit the tee with the driver head, and you will hear a noise from the contact. If you miss the tee you know that your swing was either too upright or too far off the correct swing path. If you miss the tee or do not hear a sound on your backswing, stop your swing and start over at address. Keep practicing this drill until you can hit the tee easily each time on your backswing. Your swing thought as you practice this drill should be "extend" or "reach."

Step 3: Move The Tee Farther Back

Once you are comfortable with the initial drill, begin to move the tee back farther away from the ball in half-inch increments. Keep moving the tee back until you can no longer hit the tee on your backswing without a significant lunge or spine angle change.

In the Tee Back drill it is acceptable (and even recommended) to allow your upper body to move slightly backward on the backswing. Again, your head and shoulders may move to the right as much as 2 or 3 inches to facilitate your weight shift.

The key is to allow your weight to move backward but still retain your leverage position. If you find that your lateral upper body movement is causing you to become flat-footed or even to allow your weight to roll to the outside of your right foot, shorten up the Tee Back position until you can make good extension and still maintain your leverage.

Once you can consistently hit the tee, start moving the tee back in half-inch increments until you cannot hit the tee without lunging or sliding back. Move the tee a half-inch closer to the ball from that point and practice with the tee in that location until you can consistently hit the tee on your backswing.

Once you are consistently hitting the tee from the farthest position back, begin moving the tee even farther back. This drill is like stretching muscles. At first you may be tight and unable to extend very far back. But as you reach your initial maximum extension distance and become consistent at that width, you will discover that you can add another inch or two to your swing width over time.

This process may take several weeks for you to find your true maximum extension, so you want to work on gradually extending your swing within the boundaries of balance, leverage, and control.

Variation: Combine The Slant Board With The Tee Back Drill

As you practice the Tee Back drill your goal is to make your swing as wide as possible without losing your leverage point. To help you retain your weight on the inside part of the ball of your right foot you can combine the Tee Back drill with the Slant Board drill. Your swing thought and focus will still be on generating a wide swing, but the slant board swing aid can help you avoid losing your leverage position.

Select "Swing Arc" on the main menu of the accompanying DVD to view the Tee Back drill. Or you can find the drill online at: http://www.targetcenteredgolf.com/tee_back.html

Swing Arc Drill #3: Parallel Clubs

Purpose
Encourage extension and swing plane.

Use parallel clubs to determine the take-away path and as a visual for the follow-through.

Correct backswing should be on plane, which means slightly inside (when viewed from directly behind) on take-away following the arc.

Parallel clubs will help you see when the club starts back on an outside path.

Parallel clubs also show you a path too far inside on the take-away.

Swing Thought
Straight Back.

Short Description Parallel Clubs Drill
Use two old shafts or two clubs from your bag. Lay them on the ground parallel to each other, anywhere from 5 inches to 10 inches apart, depending on your comfort zone. Line up the two clubs like railroad tracks so the middle is aimed directly at your target. Tee up a ball toward the front end of the two shafts. On the backswing keep the club between the two shafts for as long as possible. It should look to you as if the club is pointed to the middle of the two shafts for the first

half or more of your backswing. If you were to extend the two shafts backward for 20 feet and then stop your swing rotation when your hands got just past your belt level and look to see where the club is pointed, it should still point to the middle of the extended clubs. This drill helps with extension, swing plane, and ultimately with center face square contact.

Long Description Parallel Clubs Drill

Use the Parallel Clubs drill to help you keep the club on plane as you work to extend your swing arc. You will derive two benefits from using this drill. First, your club will remain on plane longer, which will increase your swing efficiency. Second, the parallel clubs will address the tendency to swing the club to the inside, which creates either a flat swing or a loop. A third benefit is that use of the parallel clubs makes it easy to see how square your club face is at address.

Set Up For The Parallel Club Drill

Use two old shafts or two clubs from your bag. Lay the two clubs on the ground parallel to each other, anywhere from 5 inches to 10 inches apart, depending on your comfort zone. Line up the two clubs like railroad tracks so the middle area between the clubs is aimed directly at your target. The closer the clubs are to each other, the smaller your margin for error. Thus, start off learning this drill with plenty of room between the shafts. As you get better at this drill, keep moving the clubs closer together to challenge yourself to improve your swing path and accuracy.

Tee up a ball toward the forward end of the two shafts. You want as much of the shafts behind the ball as possible because you will be using them as a visual aid for your takeaway.

On your backswing your goal is to keep your driver between the two shafts for as long as possible on the takeaway. This is a good training aid set-up to use with the Tee Back drill as well.

Take several practice backswings and watch the path of your clubhead during the backswing. Imagine the two shafts are like railroad tracks that extend straight back for 20 or 30 feet. If you are keeping your head steady and watching the driver head on your practice swings, it should appear to you that the club points continuously to the middle area of the two extended shafts until your hands get just above your belt level.

Stop your swing rotation when your hands are just past your belt level and look to see where the club is pointed. Your driver should still point to the middle of the extended clubs. This drill helps with extension, swing plane, and ultimately with center face square contact.

Select "Swing Arc" on the main menu of the accompanying DVD to view the Parallel Clubs drill. Or you can find the drill online at: http://www.targetcenteredgolf.com/parallel_clubs.html

8

DISTANCE KEY #4: SPEED OF HIPS

Recall that the 3 swing factors that affect distance are Speed (clubhead speed at impact), Centeredness (square clubface, middle contact at impact); and Angle of Approach.

Hip speed is your key to clubhead speed. The faster you can rotate your hips to the target, the faster your club will move. Anything you can do to increase hip speed (while still maintaining balance and leverage) will help you drive the ball farther.

A good hip turn allows your lower body rotation to bring the club into the hitting position and helps preserve lag. Throwing your club at the ball from the top or dropping your arms down before the lower body has rotated will cause you to lose lag and develop a power leak.

Develop your hip speed to get the club back to the ball with maximum clubhead speed at and through the ball.

Imagine your downswing as unwinding from the ground up. Your feet and legs begin to drive and rotate toward the target. Your legs carry your hips through to the target. Your hips lead your shoulders, and your shoulders lead your arms. Your hands and the club come through the impact zone last, like the crack of a whip.

The "X-Factor" Myth

The X-Factor was all the rage for several years, and I continue to field questions about it from students. In essence, the X-Factor was a measure of how much farther your shoulders rotated back than your hips during the backswing. The idea was that the greater the differential between your shoulder rotation and your hip rotation the more power you would store in your backswing. If you could keep your hips dead still during the backswing and rotate your shoulders 90 degrees you would have a maximum X-Factor.

It doesn't work.

The reason is relatively straightforward. The X-Factor will cause you to unwind from the top down. Your shoulders (since they have turned the farthest away from the ball), will initiate the downswing while your hips remain locked in place. By the time your shoulders get square to your hips, any X-Factor power you created during your backswing will be gone. You will have accelerated TO the ball, and almost invariably your hands will release about waist-high—far too early to deliver clubhead speed THROUGH the ball.

The X-Factor power you create during your backswing makes absolutely no difference during your downswing.

The only time the X-Factor does make a difference is on the downswing itself. Let me explain.

On the downswing you want your hips to lead your shoulders toward the target. You want to unwind your downswing from the ground up. The longer you can keep your hips ahead of your shoulders through impact, the more torque your core will develop, and the more swing speed you will deliver through the ball.

If you make a proper pivot you will deliver the club consistently square at impact with maximum clubhead speed. Here is how my swing has changed to both deliver clubhead speed as well as protect my back.

Stack Your Hips Over Your Knee

As mentioned earlier, one of the key swing changes I made to help improve swing speed as well as eliminate the risk of lower back injury was to flatten out my belt angle during the swing.

Imagine holding a 20-foot piece of pvc pipe right on top of your belt at address. If your hips are level at address the pipe will be parallel to the ground and extend out to either side of you by nearly 10 feet.

Now imagine making a swing so the far ends of the pipe stay level with the ground throughout the swing, never touching the ground. Your belt would have to remain level throughout the swing to keep the pipe level.

Compare the visualization of this swing to your current swing. Most of my students initially dip their left hip down toward the ball on the backswing. Since golf tends to be an action/counter-action movement, the left hip dip usually results in a counter-acting right hip dip (or left hip upward thrust) on the downswing. This motion describes the classic "Reverse C" swing position.

I believe the modern swing is moving substantially away from the Reverse C and moving toward a flatter belt line with a more vertical spine throughout the swing. The flatter hip line and straighter spine angle will protect your back.

Annika Sorenstam—The Swing Of The Future

I am sure you've had a chance to observe LPGA champion Annika Sorenstam. Her swing may be the swing of the future (other than the look-away* at impact). At address she is athletically balanced, and during the swing she remains athletically centered. On the backswing her hip line remains level. Her left heel lifts off the ground to facilitate this level hip turn. She initiates her downswing by planting her left heel and rotating her hips evenly through to the finish, where she remains in athletic balance. She has no spine angle change during the swing, which contributes tremendously to her consistency.

Annika's swing is simple, consistent, and biomechanically efficient. Almost everybody can make the same kind of swing as Annika, whereas not everybody is physically capable of making the classic Reverse C swing.

Her swing also has tremendous power because she makes such good use of her leverage position and her core muscle strength. It looks effortless because she is not working hard with her hands and arms attempting to generate clubhead speed.

She is generating her speed with her hips from a highly leveraged position. She creates a single leverage axis that runs in a straight line from the ball of her right foot through her knee to her center of mass. It is a very solid, very powerful position at the top of the backswing, yet it is not full of tension.

(*Annika's look-away: At impact Annika's head is rotated toward the target and her eyes are clearly in front of the ball. She is "looking away" from the ball. My understanding is that this look-away started off as a drill for her to help her finish toward the target. The drill worked so well and she practiced it so much that it became a part of her normal swing. The look-away is her unique quirk, and we all have them. Remember, the key is to do what works for YOU. I don't recommend the look-away except as a drill, but that aside, her swing is well worth emulating.)

HIP SPEED DRILLS

Hip Speed Drill #1: Sole Plant
Hip Speed Drill #2: Baseball Stride
Hip Speed Drill #3: Heel Plant

Here are a series of drills to help develop hip speed. To view all the Speed Drills select "Hip Speed" from the main menu of the accompanying DVD.

Hip Speed Drill #1: Sole Plant

Purpose

Develop hip speed.

Swing Thought

Hips.

Short Description Sole Plant Drill

The Sole Plant drill involves turning your belt buckle 90 degrees away from the ball at the top of the swing and allowing your left foot to roll up so your left toe is completely pointed at the ground and the sole of your left shoe is facing toward the target. There should be no weight on your left foot. Initiate the downswing by imagining a tee lying sideways on the ground that you are going to break in half with your left heel.

Use the forceful left heel plant to create your fastest hip rotation so you finish your swing with your belt buckle completely facing the target and all of your weight on your left foot. This drill has considerably more hip rotation than you would expect in your normal swing. In fact, the drill is much like the Baseball Rip Swing that you learned in the balance section, except that in this case you will be hitting a ball. You should also not worry about your leverage position with this drill. Your primary focus will be on hip speed.

Long Description Sole Plant Drill

The concept behind the Sole Plant drill is to develop as much hip speed as possible by maximizing the amount of overall hip rotation back and forward. Your goal will be to turn your hips as far away from the ball on the backswing as possible, and then from that position, turn your hips to the target as fast as possible, while hitting the golf ball.

Step 1: 90° Backswing Hip Rotation

Take your normal stance and posture and address a ball. On your backswing turn your hips 90 degrees away from the ball so your belt buckle (which started facing the ball) is facing right, directly away from the target.

In order to reach this backswing position you will need to allow your left leg to relax so your left shoe can roll all the way up and the toe can point to the ground without any weight on it. All of your weight should be on your right side.

This part of the Sole Plant drill is very similar to the Baseball Rip drill in that the first few times you attempt to complete this backswing your hips and left foot will likely only get ½ to ¾ of the way back. It will probably take several practice swings before you can successfully make this 90 degree backswing as well as allow your left toe to point into the ground.

Please pay attention during this process not just to getting to the right position, but also to what muscle groups you had to relax to achieve this exaggerated turn.

When you get to this extreme backswing position your weight will be over the top of, or on the outside part of your right foot. Once again, you don't need to worry about your leverage position with this drill. Simply concentrate on hip speed. Move your hips as much as possible.

Step 2: Downswing Hip Speed

Initiate the downswing by forcefully planting your left heel on the ground and allowing the force of the heel plant to pivot your hips toward the target. Your goal is to get your belt buckle facing the target as quickly as possible.

You may try imagining a tee lying sideways on the ground under the outside portion of your left heel—about where your ankle is located. As you make your backswing and then start your downswing, try to break the tee in half with the outside edge of your left foot. In order to break the tee with the outside part of your left foot you will need to shift your weight to your left side. Placing the tee outside and back toward your ankle will help ensure you make a pivot as you accomplish this weight shift, rather than a hip slide.

Step 3: Releasing The Club Tension Free

During this swing you will be generating as much hip speed and clubhead speed as possible. It is less important where the ball goes, particularly when you first attempt this drill. Your emphasis during the swing should be on staying in balance and allowing the rotation of your hips and core to generate speed for the clubhead.

Your grip pressure and arm tension should be minimal. On the 1 to 10 scale your grip pressure and tension should be 3 or lower—just enough to keep your hold on the club. Remember, you do not want tension in your hands and arms to slow down your swing.

Think crack-the-whip to generate a mental picture of how your body should be swinging the club. You want your club and your arms to lag as far behind you as possible when you execute your downswing, so the torque of your core rotation whips the club through the impact zone. You should feel as though your body is flinging the club toward the target, with almost no pressure in the hands and arms other than what is required to square up the clubhead at impact.

Step 4: Finish Your Swing

Finish your swing with your hips completely facing the target and your right toe pointed into the ground with no weight on it. Your arms and shoulders will likely over-rotate, particularly if you maintain a tension-free swing.

Select "Swing Arc" on the main menu of the accompanying DVD to view the Sole Plant drill. Or you can find the drill online at: http://www.targetcenteredgolf.com/videos/sole_plant.html

Hip Speed Drill #2: Baseball Stride Drill

Purpose

Lower body lead. Leg drive. Also helps with weight shift.

Swing Thought

Step, THEN Swing.

Short Description Baseball Stride Drill

The purpose of the Baseball Stride drill is to help you get the feel of starting your downswing with your lower body. Practicing the Baseball Stride Drill can also help with understanding proper timing. Take your normal stance and address with an iron, but move the ball up to your left foot (in the driver position). Leaving your club on the ground behind the ball, move your left foot back toward your right foot. With your feet close together complete your backswing. Pause slightly at the top, and then start your downswing by lifting your left foot and taking a baseball stride toward the target. Plant your left foot, shift your weight and make your rotation, then allow the club to swing down and hit the ball. You want to consciously hold your arms back as long as possible during this drill. Your swing thought should be "step, THEN swing" with the THEN serving as a reminder to keep your hands and arms back while your lower body completes the swing. Keep your grip pressure at 4 (on a scale of 10) or less on this drill.

Long Description Baseball Stride Drill

The Baseball Stride drill is designed to help you understand how the lower body should lead the way on the downswing. To practice this drill, imagine a baseball player at the plate. As the pitch comes in the batter shifts his weight back, then raises his left foot and steps into the pitch to make his swing. This drill makes use of the same weight transfer and sequencing of weight shift and hip turn.

Step 1: Baseball Stride Drill—Feet Together

Use an iron for this drill. Take your normal stance and address position with one exception. For this drill you will move the ball forward in your stance to your left foot, where you would normally position the ball for a driver shot. Leaving the clubhead on the ground behind the ball, move your left foot back toward your right foot so your feet are together. Your right foot does not move. You will have to reach forward to keep the clubhead behind the ball.

Step 2: Baseball Stride Drill—Step, THEN Swing

Take your normal backswing. At the top of your swing pause the club. Start your downswing by stepping forward. Plant your left foot to initiate both the weight shift and hip turn. You will complete most of your weight shift and hip turn before you allow your arms to swing down to the ball.

Your goal with the baseball stride drill is to overemphasize the initiation of the downswing with the lower body. You want to hold your arms and hands back as long as possible, while your lower body nearly completes the weight shift and hip turn, so your forward momentum and body rotation make it impossible to keep the club back any longer.

Step 3: Baseball Stride Drill—Release The Club To The Target

When your weight shift and core rotation are nearly complete, allow the momentum generated by your rotation to swing the club through the impact area. That is why the swing thought is "step, THEN swing" with the emphasis on the pause caused by the "then" cadence. Keep your grip pressure relatively light during this drill—approximately 3 or 4 (on a scale of 10) so you can feel the club release toward the target.

If you have a tendency to bring the club down early with your hands and arms, this drill will emphasize the importance of proper sequencing and timing. Many of my students challenged with this issue soon discover they are hitting the ball before their left foot has even touched the ground. When this happens the timing mismatch is easy for students to feel.

Variation 1 Baseball Stride Drill—Gary Player Walk-Through

If you have a challenge getting your lower body to lead the way on the downswing and if you have a challenge getting your weight shifted completely to your left side on the downswing, try this drill variation.

Gary Player has been a golf icon for more than half a century. If you have seen him play in the last few years you will notice one of his swing quirks—he hits the ball and then walks a few steps toward the target. Gary is so committed to getting his weight to the left side and to getting every ounce of momentum possible through the ball that his weight shift literally causes him to keep walking once he hits. There may be some benefits for you in this drill variation.

When you take your baseball stride drill, hit the ball and take a few steps toward the target. We call this the Gary Player walk-through. In order for you to take a step toward the target with your right foot after you hit, you must take all the weight off the right foot. You won't be able to take a forward step if you still have weight on your right foot after impact.

Since you are already making a step with your left foot to start the downswing, taking another step with your right foot after impact will be somewhat instinctual in that you won't have to consciously make any adjustments to keep moving. If you keep your mental focus on walking forward after impact, your body will make the necessary weight shift to prepare you for your step.

Select "Speed" on the main menu of the accompanying DVD to view the Baseball Stride drill. Or you can find the drill online at: http://www.targetcenteredgolf.com/videos/baseball_stride.html

Hip Speed Drill #3: Heel Plant Drill

Purpose
Start the downswing with the lower body and develop hip speed as well as leg drive.

Swing Thought
Stomp!

Short Description Heel Plant Drill
The Heel Plant drill is designed to help you get the feel of starting the downswing with a left side heel plant, weight shift, and pivot. On your backswing allow your left heel to rise off the ground an inch or two. Imagine a tee lying sideways on the ground underneath your left

heel, toward the outside portion of your shoe. Start your downswing by planting your left heel hard enough on the tee to break it in two. Allow the heel plant to pull the hips into a pivot, so your weight shift and pivot are happening as a result of your foot driving down. Your swing thought is "stomp" or break the tee. Keep your grip pressure under 4 (on a scale of 10) and allow the club to swing through the impact area as rapidly as possible.

Long Description Heel Plant Drill

In his book "How I play Golf" Tiger Woods notes that when he wants a little more distance he "snaps" his left knee straight on the downswing. That move allows him to clear his hips faster, which in turn speeds up the rotation of his shoulders and ultimately his arms and the club.

The Heel Plant drill works in much the same manner, but with less risk to your knee (perhaps the "snap" is why Tiger has so much knee trouble. He should try this heel plant instead).

Step 1 Heel Plant Drill—Lift the Left Heel

Take your normal address position with the driver. On your backswing allow your left heel to come off the ground a couple of inches during your rotation. Allowing your heel to come off the ground should facilitate more hip rotation on the backswing, giving you a better "wind up" as you store power for the downswing. The other benefit of allowing the left heel to rise is that it is much easier to keep your belt line level, which means you will be putting considerably less torque on your lower back.

Step 2 Heel Plant Drill—Plant and Rotate

Pause at the top of the backswing to "set" the club, and then start your downswing by driving your left heel into the ground. You don't want to create any extra lateral motion with the hips, so when you plant the left heel use that momentum to facilitate your hip rotation at the same time.

When you make your heel plant you want to focus on getting your weight on the outside part of your left foot in the area of your ankle. To emphasize the position of where your weight should come down you can lay a tee down on the ground underneath your left ankle on the outer part of the shoe. Then, try to break the tee in half when you plant your heel on the downswing.

Students sometimes practice just the heel plant part a couple of times without swinging a club until they get a sense of how to drive their left leg forcefully into the ground. Because the tee is under the outside part of their shoe they have to get their weight all the way over to the outside part of their foot before they can create enough force to try to break the tee. If you plant your heel on the inside part of your left foot you won't facilitate any kind of hip rotation.

Once students get the idea of forcefully planting their left foot they work next to integrate hip rotation into that movement. The heel plant alone won't generate clubhead speed at impact unless it is used to create hip rotation.

Step 3 Heel Plant Drill—Finish With A Handshake

To paint a picture for my students I have them imagine a simple hand shake.

I have them turn away in their backswing (without a club) with their heel off the ground. I take up a position about 3 feet to their left and down their target line. From their position at the top I have them simply turn toward me and reach out with their right hand to shake hands.

This is a completely natural motion for most people, and they invariably do it in exactly the right sequence without having to focus on the mechanics. From their position at the top (turned away from me), they have one simple goal (swing thought) which is to shake hands. They let their body figure out how to get them to the right position.

They plant their left heel first and simultaneously initiate a weight shift together with hip rotation. Because they know they will have to reach out for my hand (target extension), they naturally shift their weight to the outside part of their left foot, and they position their center of mass straight over their ankle so they end up in a balanced position. Their right hand swings up and out in a natural movement.

When you practice your Heel Plant drills keep these visual images of breaking the tee and shaking hands in mind.

Variation 1 Heel Plant Drill: Right Knee Kick

This is a variation on the Heel Plant drill that actually focuses on your right side to achieve the same hip turn and weight shift as the Heel Plant drill. It is in many respects similar to the Gary Player Walk-through, but in this case you won't be taking any additional steps.

As you make your downswing and continue your rotation through impact kick your right knee forcibly toward the target. When my wife took a self-defense class they taught her how to disable an attacker by delivering a sharp knee blow to the man's groin area. (Fortunately she did not require that I practice this defensive move with her.) But the idea is the same: Kicking your right knee toward the target requires the two things you are practicing with these drills—a weight shift and a fast hip turn.

Variation 2 Heel Plant Drill: Right Heel Fire

The Right Heel Fire is very similar to the Right Knee Kick drill variation since it focuses on the right side to generate hip speed. I came up with this drill while working with a student who had bad knees, and it has worked successfully for a number of other students as well.

Because my student with the bad knees couldn't effectively drive with his legs we had to come up with another way for him to generate hip speed without risking additional physical damage. The answer was to focus on firing the right heel on the downswing.

The goal with this drill is to get your right heel up in the air with your shoelaces pointed at the target as quickly as possible on the downswing. Keeping this swing thought in mind will force you to get your weight off your right foot quickly. If you get your right heel in the air fast enough it will force your left side to rotate and get out of the way in a hurry.

With both the Knee Kick drill and the Right Heel Fire drill you will want to keep your hands relatively light on the club, with a grip pressure of only 3 or 4 (on a scale of 10). You want to develop the feel of a fast hip turn whipping the club through the impact area, and you can only accomplish this with less hand and arm tension.

Select "Speed" on the main menu of the accompanying DVD to view the Heel Plant drill. Or you can find the drill online at: http://www.targetcenteredgolf.com/videos/heel_plant.html

9

DISTANCE KEY #5: TARGET EXTENSION

Last in the B.L.A.S.T. progression is extension to the target.

Being able to extend the club to the target ensures that you maintain clubhead speed *through* the ball, not just to the ball. Far too many golfers inadvertently accelerate their club TO the ball. The result is an early release of lag, which means that the club will be traveling the fastest around your waist, not at the ball. This is different from casting, where the clubhead starts down from the top of the swing toward the ball first before your body starts rotating, causing you to lose most of your lag position at the top of the swing.

When golfers accelerate TO the ball instead of THROUGH the ball they tend to stop their hip rotation *at the ball.*

Whenever your hips stop rotating, your hands release.

Since your hips are usually leading the arms in the downswing, when the hips stop, the hands will release anywhere from your hips to the right thigh. The result will be a flip of the club, meaning that the left wrist will cup. From there the ball can go just about anywhere—a thin shot to a top, a nasty hook, or a shank.

For this reason I don't like the old adage of "feel as if you are sitting on a stool" on the downswing. Sitting on a stool means your hips have stopped rotating. That seldom results in a consistent golf shot with power.

Extension Drills

Select "Target Extension" on the main menu of the accompanying DVD to view the Target Extension drills. Or you can find the drills online at: http://www.targetcenteredgolf.com/videos/tee_forward.html

Extension Drill #1: Tee Forward
Extension Drill #2: High Finish
Extension Drill #3: Tension Free Swing

Extension Drill #1: Tee Forward

Purpose

Extension through the ball.

Swing Thought

Extend.

Short Description Tee Forward Drill

Use the Tee Forward drill to maintain a target focus so your club continues to accelerate through the impact zone toward the target. Place a tee in the ground a foot or two in front of your ball. Just before you swing imagine that the ball is located on the forward tee so that you will have to accelerate through the impact zone and reach to hit the forward tee. Your swing thought should be "extend" or reach. You don't necessarily have to hit the forward tee. It is more important to focus on extending your club toward the target. You don't want your right arm to completely straighten out until the clubhead passes the second tee.

Long Description Tee Forward Drill

Without a target focus your attention will naturally turn to the ball and you will accelerate your club **to** the ball, instead of **through** the ball to the target. By the time your clubhead gets to the ball you will have spent much of your clubhead speed halfway through the downswing. The Tee Forward drill shifts the focus of your swing to a spot forward of the ball.

This shift of focus helps with multiple desirable components of a fast swing. First, it will help you transfer your weight to your left side more effectively on the downswing because your body knows instinctively that to hit a target farther forward it will have to be farther forward to reach the target.

Second, focusing on hitting the forward tee will help keep your right elbow bent and in a power position longer. If you analyze the swing of nearly any PGA Tour professional and focus on the right arm position at impact you will observe that the right elbow still has a bend in it when the clubhead makes contact with the ball. The right arm does not straighten out until *after* impact.

Yet, if you did the same slow motion analysis of most weekend golfers you would find that their right arm straightens out well before the bottom of the swing, and in most cases well before impact. When you practice the Tee Forward drill your body will recognize instinctively that there is no way the clubhead can hit the forward tee if your right arm has straightened out before impact. The club will be traveling up immediately after impact and will not have the extension necessary to hit the forward tee. The club has already bottomed out and is rising upward from the point of contact with the ball.

Third, the Tee Forward drill will help you clear your hips earlier and rotate them more efficiently toward the target by the time of impact.

We already mentioned the physiological constraints on achieving any kind of arm extension toward the target if your hips are stopped at impact. If your habit is to have your hips stop rotating when they get back to square your arms will have no way to extend. You will create a chicken wing position, and you will not be able to reach the forward tee with your left elbow bending away.

The interesting correlation I have noticed with students is that when they keep their focus forward, their hips seem to turn automatically to face the forward tee on the downswing. This is a great position for the hips! On a normal shot their hip rotation stops as soon as the hips get back to square with the ball, but with a tee out front the hips have a more continuous rotation, and they rotate farther toward the target.

To practice the Tee Forward drill, place a second tee in the ground approximately 18 inches in front of your tee ball. At address you should just about (but not quite) be able to reach forward with your driver and touch the tee without moving your head or upper body. Put the tee a couple of inches in front of that spot.

During your pre-shot routine spend as much time looking at the forward tee as you spend looking at your ball. As you conduct your normal golf swing, try to hit the second tee as your club moves through the impact area. The tee should be far enough forward to cause you to reach with both arms. If you can hit the forward tee on your shot, try moving it a little farther out. Keep moving the tee farther and farther out until you reach the point where you feel as though you have to lunge or change spine angle to reach the tee. Back it up a half-inch and keep practicing. Over time you should be able to move the tee farther and farther out and still feel comfortable with your extension.

Select "Target Extension" on the main menu of the accompanying DVD to view the Tee Forward drill. Or you can find the drill online at: http://www.targetcenteredgolf.com/videos/tee_forward.html

Extension Drill #2: High Finish

Purpose
Acceleration *through* the ball to the top of the finish. Helps remove the hit impulse

Swing Thought
Reach UP!

Short Description High Finish Drill
The second extension drill is designed to refocus your attention on finishing your swing toward your target and not accelerating your clubhead just to the ball. Take your normal swing but keep your focus on the finish position of your hands and arms. Finish with both arms fully extended in front of you, reaching to the sky. If possible, keep both arms straight on your finish, just to the left side of your head. Your swing thought should be "up" or reach. Pay attention to the way this drill helps your core rotate toward the target, and how easy it is when you maintain a high finish focus to get your weight to the left side, to

have your hips finish facing the target, and to continue to accelerate the clubhead through the impact zone to the target.

Long Description High Finish Drill

When my daughter was two years old her favorite thing in the world was to have daddy pick her up when I came home from work. As soon as I came in the door she would run toward me with her arms stretched up as high as she could reach while she yelled "uppie, uppie." That is a pretty easy picture for most golfers to imagine, so around my office we now refer to the High Finish drill as the Uppie Uppie drill (it's also a great swing thought to keep when hitting out of the sand).

The essence of the Uppie Uppie drill is to finish with your hands and arms stretched out in front of you as high in the air as you can extend them. Your swing thought while swinging is "up" or finish high, and you will want to keep a clear mental picture in mind of the finish position for your arms.

It is deceptively easy to lose this high-finish mental picture when you are hitting a ball because your brain is focused on the ball during the swing. Somehow when there is a ball on the tee your natural impulse to "hit it" momentarily takes over your thought process during the downswing. This is what we refer to as a "hit impulse."

Even though you have the best of intentions during the backswing to remain focused only on your finish position, on the downswing there is something about the ball lying helplessly on the ground while we have a club in our hand and a perfect shot at the kill that seems to take over our rational thought. Perhaps it is instinct.

One of the side benefits of the High Finish drill is that it can substantially help eliminate the hit impulse by giving your body another target and mental picture on which to focus. You will find as you practice this drill that your core speed through impact will be considerably faster than a swing in which you are ball-focused.

Select "Target Extension" on the main menu of the accompanying

DVD to view the High Finish drill. Or you can find the drill online at: http://www.targetcenteredgolf.com/videos/high_finish.html

Extension Drill #3: Tension Free Swing Drill

| Power-X | Dynamic Power Axis | Tension Free Axis |

Purpose
Dynamic power in the left arm, but tension free in the right arm.

Swing Thought
Tension Free.

Short Description Tension Free Drill

The best golf swings you make can be described as tension free. Tension free swings have dynamic power in the protagonistic muscles and no tension in the antagonistic muscles. That means the left arm and right leg should be strong and in control, while the right arm and left leg remain free to move naturally with the swing. You can do this drill alone or with a partner. Prior to hitting a golf ball, allow your right arm, right shoulder, and left leg to relax with no tension. As you hit your shot, track your tension throughout the swing. Rate your ability to remain tension free during the swing on a scale of 10, with 10 being completely tension free in the antagonistic muscles. Your swing thought should be "tension free." If you are practicing with a partner, report your tension free rating and then ask your partner for his/her observation.

Pay attention to any increase in tension levels, and also pay close attention to the area of the swing where the tension appears. The three most common areas where unwanted tension creeps in are at the takeaway (when the hands grab or snatch the club), during the transition from backswing to downswing (often tempo related), and just before impact.

Long Description Tension Free Drill

My long-time friend and mentor Dr. Glen Albaugh taught me how to make tension free swings and his sage advice has added considerably to my game (see *Winning the Battle Within* at www.wbwgolf.com). Many students find that as they practice the tension free drill and begin to gain some mastery over their tension, it quickly becomes one of their favorite practice routines.

Step 1 Tension Free Drill: Start Tension Free

Take your normal stance and address. Prior to swinging perform an internal body scan and pay particular attention to your right hand, right arm, right shoulder (and the muscles in the back of your shoulder around your scapula), and to your left leg. Thinking back to the Power-X concept, these areas and muscles represent your tension-free power axis. Allow the muscles in your tension-free axis to relax just prior to swinging. Your right shoulder should be relaxed back, and your right arm should hang naturally with a slight bend.

Right Shoulder and Arm Tension Free

Step 2 Tension Free Drill: Scan While Swinging

Start your swing with the thought "tension free" and pay attention during the swing to your tension-free axis. Perform a continuous body scan while you are swinging to note any areas that experience unwanted tension.

Step 3 Tension Free Drill: Release The Club

Finish your swing tension free and allow the club to release fully to the target. Do not inhibit the release with grip or arm tension. Your arms should feel as though they flew through the impact area by themselves. Your finish should be comfortably facing your target and well-balanced.

Develop Your Self-Awareness

You will want to pay attention to two aspects of tension during your swing. First, note which areas of your body become tense. Second, notice at which point in the swing they become tense. Simply put: where and when.

Your goal, particularly in the beginning, is to develop a highly refined sense of awareness around what your body is doing during the swing. Because your awareness is so internally focused when you start practicing this drill your shots may become erratic. Remember that a successful drill is one in which you felt something or learned something, not necessarily how well the ball was struck.

After some practice you will probably notice that you have tendencies. You tend to introduce tension in the same part of the swing and it will tend to be with the same muscle group. Once you identify that particular area, you can focus much of your practice on eliminating tension at that point of your swing. Your confidence level will increase and within a short time you will be striking the ball with more consistency.

Three Areas Of Internal Focus

There are three typical areas where tension tends to creep into a swing. It may be helpful for you as you practice to confine your initial self-awareness focus to just one area at a time. In this way you will become familiar with your tendencies at the three critical junctures of the swing takeaway, transition and impact.

Takeaway

The first area of the swing to focus on is the takeaway. A very high percentage of my students take the club away with a tightening of the hands and arms—in essence "grabbing" the club on the takeaway. Conversely, the old adage "hold the grip like you are holding a bird" doesn't work for most students either. They set their initial grip pressure prior to the swing at a 2 (on a scale of 10), believing they have the concept right.

But a 2 grip pressure isn't firm enough for most golfers to have confidence in their ability to control the club or even hang on to it, so immediately on the takeaway they squeeze the grip, often bumping their grip pressure to a 6 or 8 (on a scale of 10). This sudden grip pressure change invariably affects the clubface angle as well as the swing path, often with disastrous results.

The grip pressure change at takeaway is challenging for most students to feel at first, because adding grip pressure feels like a natural way to get the club swinging. But grabbing the club at the takeaway usually shortens swing arc and tends to limit shoulder rotation, robbing you of both clubhead speed and power.

In reality the swing starts with core rotation—the shoulders and torso. The arms and club should move back because the body is rotating. This action results in the body swinging the club. Conversely, grabbing the club at the takeaway results in the club swinging the body. These are two diametrically opposed ways to swing the club, and often understanding the difference is a liberating feeling for students. Effortless power comes from allowing the body to swing the club.

To heighten your awareness of what your hands and arms are doing it may be helpful for you to close your eyes during the takeaway, allowing them to open near the top of the swing so you can pick up the ball again. Focus your attention on your grip pressure and arm tension. Everything should be consistent on the takeaway.

Transition

The second area where tension creeps in is in the transition from backswing to downswing. Again, your goal is to have zero grip pressure or tension change during the transition. Adding tension through either a grip pressure change or through right arm or right shoulder tension often results in a cast or an early release. Adding unwanted tension during the transition spends lag early and kills swing speed.

The key to eliminating grabbing or tension in the transition is to maintain your leverage position and to focus on starting the downswing with the lower body. Your goal is to have consistent grip pressure through the transition—neither relaxing the grip nor tightening it at the top.

Far too many students mistakenly believe that their hands and arms provide the speed and power in the swing. This mind-set leads to a tremendous amount of unnecessary tension on the downswing and a feeling as if you need to throw your club at the ball.

Your core supplies the power, and your lower body initiates the downswing motion. Your hands and arms are there to control the clubface—to get it back to square at impact, not to generate power or speed. Let your body do the work, and let your hands and arms release the club tension-free to the target.

Impact

The third area where unnecessary tension tends to creep into the swing is at impact (or just before impact). The most common fault is white-knuckled grip pressure with the right hand and arm. Often the right hand becomes so dominant at impact that the left hand completely relaxes during impact, resulting in cupping of the left wrist and a flip of the club.

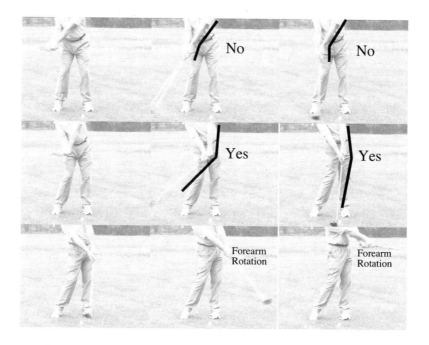

This right-hand grab is usually the easiest fault for most students to feel in their tension -free practice. The challenge is that there may be many reasons behind the tension, both mental and physical. It will be part of your practice to discover the underlying causes.

Evaluating Tension Causes

When you practice your tension free drills and you are trying to identify where and why tension creeps in, start your analysis with your mental process. In other words, once you have determined where the tension appears, ask yourself why? What are you trying to accomplish? What are your thoughts or expectations that bring about tension at this particular point in the swing?

Often you can correct a swing issue by addressing the underlying mental process and allow the mechanical issue to resolve itself. Only after you have analyzed your mental process should you then look to mechanical causes to address tension. I cover these issues in much more detail in my book *The Practice Effect: How To Groove A Reliable, Automatic Swing You Can Trust.*

Mental issues range from a lack of confidence, not knowing where the target is, trying to manipulate or steer the club, a desire for perfection, or the desire to just kill it. Physical issues may also relate to any of the four preceding Distance Keys (Balance, Leverage, Arc, Speed, and Target).

Select "Target Extension" on the main menu of the accompanying DVD to view the Tension Free drill. Or you can find the drill online at: http://www.targetcenteredgolf.com/videos/tension_free_swings.html

10

B.L.A.S.T. SUMMARY WITH DRILLS

Here are the "5 Keys to Distance" along with practical drills to help you master them. Together the 5 Keys comprise the acronym B.L.A.S.T., designed to help you remember the 5 Keys as well as the progression for mastery. It may be helpful to print this page and keep it in your golf bag to have it available for your next practice session.

Balance: Stay athletically centered over the balls of your feet.
Tight Ankles
Baseball Rip Swing
Toe Tap

Leverage: Keep your weight on the inside part of the ball of your right foot at the top of your swing.

Slant Board
Right Knee Set
Toe Press & Tee Drop

Arc Width: Generate the widest swing arc possible.

Low and Slow
Tee Back
Parallel Clubs

Speed: Your hips are the engine. Turn them as fast as possible.

Sole Plant
Baseball Stride
Heel Plant

Target Extension: Shake hands with the target and extend to the target.

Tee Forward
High Finish
Tension Free Swings

11

HOW TO PRACTICE

I was fortunate to have the opportunity to study kinesiology while I was working toward my Masters degree in Sport Psychology. An important subset of kinesiology is the study of motor learning.

Motor learning theory focuses on how we learn to move—from simple tasks like lifting a finger to complex tasks like dance or golf. I took away many keys ideas from my study of motor learning. One of the best involved the fastest way to learn new motor skills. You can think of a swing refinement as a modified motor skill.

Random Block Practice

It turns out that the fastest way to learn a new skill is through a process called "random block practice." When I learned golf I was taught that the best way to learn something was to do it over and over again. Actually, this is not the case. By now, I've done enough practicing and worked with enough students to realize that random block practice works much faster.

Practice In Blocks of 3 Or 5 Ball Sets

So here is the best way to practice, and the best way to refine a new skill: Random Block Practice. The "block" part of the term refers to how many golf balls in a row you hit. A block could be 3 or 5 balls hit in a row. "Random" refers to switching to another drill after you have hit a block of balls.

Use 3 Drills In Rotation

Generally it is better to have 3 drills grouped in a rotation all related to one of the BLAST concepts (like the three Balance drills). Hit 3 or 5 golf balls focusing on one particular drill in a B.L.A.S.T. category. Then switch to the second related drill for another 3/5 ball set. Then switch to the third related drill. Hit that set of practice balls. Then, the rotation comes back around to the first drill.

For instance, the three drills grouped under "Balance" are Tight Ankles, Baseball Rip Swing, and Toe Tap. Begin your practice with a 3 or 5 ball set of Tight Ankles shots. Then switch to Baseball Rip practice swings for the next 3 or 5 balls. Then switch to the Toe Tap drill for 3 or 5 balls. Once you are done, go back to Tight Ankles and start over with the rotation.

This is the reason you have at least 3 drills associated with each of the 5 B.L.A.S.T. concepts. The drills address related aspects of the BLAST concept you are mastering. Practicing them together in a random block practice format will accelerate your learning.

Once again, I should point out that the steps in this book are organized in a specific progression. You will benefit the most by mastering each step of the B.L.A.S.T. keys in order.

Emphasize One B.L.A.S.T. Key At A Time

When you focus on a particular B.L.A.S.T. concept you want to emphasize the drills associated with that section.

Start with Balance. Spend the majority of your effort in your first few practice sessions on the Balance drills—as much as 50% to 75% of your practice time—until you master Balance. Once you are comfortable with Balance you can move on and focus as much as 75% of your practice time on Leverage. Once you begin to master Leverage, work on your Swing Arc, then your Speed, then your Target Extension.

For example, if you are going to hit 80 golf balls in your first practice session, 60 of those shots should be dedicated to the Balance drills. With 60 golf balls you would have the equivalent of 12 five-ball sets of drills. That many sets would allow you to rotate through each of the three Balance drills four times. That's a pretty good practice session.

Use the remaining 20 balls to work on other drills related to other BLAST keys, or on integrating the drills into your regular swing. (For a comprehensive discussion of accelerated practice techniques and effectively integrating refinements into your swing see my book ***The Practice Effect:*** *How To Groove A Reliable, Consistent Golf Swing You Can Trust.*

The Progression Is Important

If you try to master hip speed before you have mastered balance and leverage, you are likely to slow your learning and spray the ball all over the place. Remember, it is hard to score from the weeds, no matter how far you are hitting it.

So stay with the progression. It is organized in a very specific sequence of steps, for good reasons. In fact, this is exactly the progression I undertake when I train to compete in long drive championships. It works for me, and I know it will work for you.

12

NOTES ABOUT THE SWING

Now that you have read the sequence of steps, seen the drills, and learned a little more about how to practice, it's time to talk in a little more detail about certain aspects of the swing and address common questions. Think of this as the FAQ section.

I'm going to start with the set up and progress through the swing in the order in which you would hit a ball. That should provide some context for where and when to consider these specific aspects of good golf swings. Some mechanical swing aspects will be more important to you than others. Some suggestions will work better than others. That's ok.

No two swings are exactly alike, so it is more important for you to do "what works" than it is for you to do what is "correct."

Let's start with the set up.

Ball Position: Forward Or Regular Position? Regular Height Or Teed Up Higher?

The traditional set up for the driver is to have the ball teed up forward in the stance at a point just inside the left foot. If you were to draw a perpendicular line from the golf ball to your feet the line would intersect your left foot at about the arch of your foot, assuming the left toe is turned slightly out toward the target.

The tee height depends on the depth of your driver face. As a rule of thumb the ball should be teed up just high enough so that when the driver is on the ground at address, **half the ball** should be above the top line of the driver face. A driver with a very low profile head—a face only 1 and 1/2 inches tall—will require the ball to be teed lower. Some of the modern 460 cc drivers have a deep face—as much as 2 and 1/4 inches tall—and will require the ball to be teed up ¾ inch higher than the low profile head. This will ensure that half the ball is above the top of the driver head.

Most professional long drivers tee the ball up higher and move the ball forward in the stance. The purpose is to hit the ball more on the upswing. But remember that long drivers are using drivers with only 5 or 6 degrees of loft, so to get a launch angle of 18 degrees they need an approach angle of 12 to 13 degrees—4 or 5 degrees more than traditional lofted drivers. The idea is that the most perfectly square hit you can put on the ball (your launch angle) will match the combined total of your approach angle plus the club loft.

Most golfers using a 9 or 10 degree driver will have more success achieving more carry distance by moving the ball only slightly forward in their stance, but not more than the width of one ball. They will also get a little more carry by teeing the ball up slightly higher, but not much more than ½ inch. If you move the ball too far forward and tee it too high you will hit too much on the upswing, hitting balloon balls with too much spin that drop out of the sky and don't release forward.

You are trying to hit balls that have a spin rate of 2,500 to 3,000 rpm with a slightly flatter (or parabolic) trajectory, as opposed to a trajectory that causes the ball to fly straight up and come straight down. A ball with a parabolic flight will land and release forward, whereas a balloon or a climbing trajectory won't roll out.

The Takeaway: Cock The Wrists Early Or Late?

The reason I believe in postponing the wrist cock on the takeaway is that a one-piece takeaway promotes better core rotation away from the ball as well as a longer swing arc. I also believe it improves synchronization of the swing because it gives your body more time to get in the right position on the back swing.

In my experience, the earlier you cock your wrists on the backswing, the earlier you release your hands on the downswing. Since the primary point of this book is to maximize your swing speed at the point of impact, anything you do that causes you to release your hands early and lose lag is counterproductive. I'm sure you have noticed by now that it is nearly impossible to implement the tee-back drill if you load your wrists early.

The key issue for me, and the challenge for most golfers, is to have quiet hands on the takeaway, achieve good extension on the backswing, but still have the right elbow soft enough so it folds into the right position at the top of the swing. If the right elbow is too stiff or straight on the backswing then you can end up with a flying right elbow at the top, or a right elbow that is behind the chest and shoulders at the top. Most of the time, this will result in an outside-in or over-the-top downswing. Ideally the right forearm will be close to vertical at the top of the swing and the right elbow will be even with the plane of your chest not behind the chest.

Turn The Hips Back Or Keep Them Still?

This is the "X-Factor" question, and I must confess that the idea of immobilizing the hips and maximizing the shoulder turn relative to the hips on the backswing has ruined a lot of swings. It's crazy. The X-Factor on the backswing is irrelevant, because you aren't hitting the ball on your backswing. For the average golfer all it does is produce an arm swing, which results in a huge power loss, no distance, and inconsistency.

The only place you want to maximize your hip turn relative to the shoulders is on the downswing. That's where the true X-Factor is. Even the professional Tour players you watch on TV who have learned to swing without much backward hip rotation on the backswing still have learned to lead the downswing with the lower body and to rotate the hips well in advance of the shoulders.

Your body core is much stronger than your arms. If you are not using your core you are giving away distance and probably producing a tension-filled swing that leaves you exhausted at the end of a round.

The drills and exercises in this book are designed to get you using your core in an efficient and naturally athletic way. The best drivers of the ball have their hips nearly turned to the target at impact. It is far simpler to have a good turn forward if you have a good turn back. Think of it as action/reaction. The farther you stretch a rubber band back, the faster it will snap forward. You will have a far easier time generating clubhead speed if your hips are moving faster.

The hips are the engine of the swing. Jason Zuback, one of the legends of long drive and a 5-time winner of the world long drive championship, has an extreme hip movement. His unique move is the secret to his remarkable distance and consistency.

When Jason takes his backswing, his hips are turned 90 degrees away from the ball! His hips have to travel 180 degrees to get to the target on the downswing, and because he does this so quickly the club has no choice but to follow along at 145+ mph.

Allow your hips to move back away from the ball on your backswing. The caveat I must add is that you MUST maintain your leverage position on the inside part of the ball of your right foot. Otherwise, you will have a sway with too much lateral hip movement.

You are trying to accomplish a pivot, and the old adage about feeling like you are swinging inside of a barrel is a good image to keep in mind. The golf swing takes place between the insides of the feet, not the outside of the feet. If you can get a good 30 to 40 degree turn away from the ball you should be in great position to make the best use of your core strength and generate hip speed.

Lift The Left Heel Or Keep It Down?

The most common question I get regarding the mechanics of generating swing speed deals with lifting the left foot on the backswing. Should you lift your left heel?

Keep in mind what we are tenaciously attempting to do. We are generating maximum clubhead speed through impact. The engine for your speed is your hips, not your shoulders, not your arms, and not your hands. Hip speed is the primary factor for generating reliable swing speed.

It is possible to keep your left heel planted and still make a good hip turn back. You must maintain good flexibility to accomplish this move. If you do not have great flexibility you should probably allow the left heel to come up, and this is particularly true as we get older.

If you get a chance to study some of golf's all time greatest swings you will see that many of these players lifted their left heel. Bobby Jones, Sam Snead, Byron Nelson to name just a few. Today's teachers have the left heel planted on the ground. But I believe the heel lift trend is coming around again, and the swing of the future will have the heel coming up with the driver (like Annika Sorenstam).

One of the benefits of allowing the left heel to come up is that it enables you to maintain a flatter belt angle throughout the swing. This eliminates the old reverse "C" move that causes so many lower back problems. I believe Annika Sorenstam's swing is very nearly the prototype of the swing of the future. Her heel comes up on her drive swing and her hips remain relatively flat during the swing. This produces very little rotational stress on the lower back and at the same time helps her generate a powerful and consistent swing.

In my own swing, the left heel comes off the ground an inch or two on my drives, a little with my 5 iron, and not at all on my wedge shots. As the clubs get shorter and shorter my left heel moves less and less, because with a wedge I am not really interested in power as much as I am in control and accuracy.

Head Movement: Steady Or Moving With The Swing?

Having studied kinesiology and motor movement, and having worked with biomechanical movement specialists, I think the answer unequivocally is that with the driver the upper body should shift slightly to the right on the backswing. This movement (and we are talking about only 2-3 inches), facilitates a weight shift into the right side, where you are storing power for the swing. On the downswing the upper body should shift back to the left so the head ends up back in its original starting position.

Under no circumstances should your head elevation change, nor should your head move inward toward the ball, or back away from the ball (these are actually spine angle changes).

13

HOW TO CREATE A RELIABLE PRE-SHOT ROUTINE

The last two parts of the puzzle—the pre-shot routine and the post-shot routine—will help make your swing as automatic and reliable as possible.

While a pre-shot routine won't guarantee you'll hit a perfect shot each time, it will consistently set you up in the best position to hit the shot you envision.

Similarly, the post-shot routine can help you quickly refocus and even right the ship when it feels as though you may be headed off course during a round. It will also be one of your key tools to use on the range to help you learn more and refine your mechanics faster with each shot.

The best place to create and refine your pre- and post-shot routines is on the range. You'll want to practice both routines with the same kind of deliberate focus and intent that you apply to learning and refining mechanical technique, so that by the time you take them to the course they feel completely automatic and natural.

The Pre-Shot Routine

We'd all like to play more consistent golf. We'd all like our swings to be more reliable. It makes sense, then, to use any and all means at our disposal to help you achieve these goals.

If you don't have or don't use a pre-shot routine on every shot then you are not using all the tools available to you to stack the odds in your favor.

On the PGA Tour 100% of the players use a pre-shot routine, whereas, in my experience, fewer than 20% of amateur players have and consistently use a pre-shot routine. The better the player, the more likely they use a pre-shot routine. Why not create and use a pre-shot routine now and get better faster?

Benefits of Using A Pre-Shot Routine

A serviceable pre-shot routine is easy to create and implement, and using it is completely within your control. To put it simply, a pre-shot routine consists of the things you habitually do prior to each swing to get into position to make the shot. A well-defined and consistently practiced pre-shot routine will incorporate the same steps, in the same order, at the same tempo, for each swing, every time.

Implementing a pre-shot routine will help you: 1) feel more comfortable over each shot; 2) focus on the appropriate objectives; 3) eliminate unnecessary mental chatter or indecision; and 4) establish and maintain good rhythm and tempo.

Your pre-shot routine should uniquely suite your game. Moreover, as your game changes your pre-shot routine will change with your game. Plus there will be times when one aspect of your swing either needs extra attention or is working particularly well. Your pre-shot routine will help you put the most effective steps on automatic while providing a consistent reminder of the parts that need attention.

To help you get started writing down your own pre-shot routine I've created an outline below. The outline doesn't cover all of the aspects or details of a pre-shot routine, but it should give you a jump start. If you already have a pre-shot routine, this information may help you analyze your current routine to be sure you are including all the elements you need.

Specifically, you will note that I recommend incorporating some of the elements of the drills and swing thoughts from the B.L.A.S.T. concepts. Use the keys that work best for you and the specific swing thoughts associated with them. Make them as automatic as possible during practice, so you don't have to think about them during the swing.

Don't be afraid to experiment and to change. Your routine will evolve just as your game will evolve. The point is to create a routine that works effectively and reliably for you and puts your swing on automatic

I highly recommend you write down your pre-shot routine step-by-step and then practice it as often as possible—preferably with every shot! Even on the range!

Creating Your Own Pre-Shot Routine

I use a small notebook in which I write down a key word that represents each major step of my routine. I place the notebook close to the ball so I can see it as I prepare to hit a shot. I go through each step as written, often saying the key words out loud as I progress through each step. If you practice your routine often enough the steps blend together so the whole routine takes 8 to 12 seconds behind the ball, and only 4 to 7 seconds once you are over the ball.

For example, my routine starts when I am standing behind the ball looking at my target. I use my imagination to picture how the ball will fly to the target, where it will land, and how it will roll out once it hits the ground. Sometimes the mental picture comes right away. Sometimes I have to experiment with different mental pictures until something feels right. But I don't move on to the next step in my routine—my rehearsal swings—until I have that clear picture in my mind.

The whole first step is summarized in my notebook by the keyword "see it." I don't have to write out in long hand a complete description of the process I use to "see it." The process will be a little different on each shot because the circumstances will be a little different each time and conjuring the mental picture may take a little more or a little less time. It is enough to have the keyword reminder because I always end up in the same place—"seeing" a mental picture of the shot.

Your pre-shot routine starter kit is below. I've outlined the major steps. Each step has a short description followed by the keyword that summarizes the step. In the section following the description you will find the list of keywords showing how I would write them down in my notebook and repeat out loud as I practiced the routine.

Pre-Shot Routine Starter Kit

Step 1: Stand behind the ball looking at the target. Assess the situation. Begin to form a mental picture of the shot you want to hit. Start to focus. Keyword: "See it."

Step 2: Breathe and relax. Take practice "rehearsal" swings to match the feel of the club swinging to what you see. Keyword: "Feel it."

Step 3: Approach the ball. Keep your eyes on the target. Establish your line as well as your tempo in the pace of your steps. Keyword: "Target Line"

Step 4: Square up to your line. Square up the club face first, then your body. Maintain your target focus. Keyword: "Line Up."

Step 5: Balance and posture check. Get comfortably athletic and ready to move in good balance. Keyword: "Balance & Posture."

Step 6: Power-X axis check. Left arm straight and powerful, right knee turned slightly in and leverage set. Right arm/left leg tension free. Get into a dynamic position ready to swing. Keyword: "Ready."

Step 7: Happy toes balance check and last look at the target. Keyword: "Target."

Step 8: Swing! Keyword: "Trust it!"

Pre-Shot Routine Keyword Summary

In my notebook this whole process is written down with just the keywords, looking something like this:

- SEE IT
- FEEL IT
- TARGET LINE
- LINE UP
- BALANCE & POSTURE
- READY
- TARGET
- TRUST IT!

(By the way, I write the keywords in large block letters so I can read them even while I am over the ball and the notebook is a few inches outside of my ball on the ground).

Try this sample pre-shot routine. It's a good place to start. Feel free to experiment, add, drop, or change the order of any element in the routine. The main goal is to develop a routine that works for you, feels comfortable, and helps your game.

The Post-Shot Routine

The next step in permanently improving your game and your swing is to develop a consistent post-shot routine.

Like the pre-shot routine, the post-shot routine focuses your observation and awareness on a series of steps and checkpoints. Again, you will pick and choose the specific steps and checkpoints that work best for you. With a little practice you will learn to complete the post-shot routine very quickly after each shot.

The idea is to compare what actually happened during your shot with what you intended to happen. If there was a difference, you want to know why. And if the results of the shot matched what you intended, you want to reinforce that process.

You've probably seen PGA tour pros on TV execute the post-shot routine—particularly after an errant shot. The pro hits a shot, evaluates the results, then steps back to make a number of corrective rehearsal swings. They do it right away, before the memory of the swing fades.

In essence, they are undergoing a rapid error-detection/error-correction process designed to understand the underlying mental or physical issue that just occurred in the swing, while simultaneously reinforcing the correct swing process prior to proceeding to the next shot. The post-shot routine puts them in a better position to get the results they want on the next shot.

Benefits Of A Post-Shot Routine

Systematizing your post-shot routine will help you learn faster on the range and adjust or adapt your performance much more quickly on the course.

The benefit to using a post-shot routine on the course is that you address mistakes immediately. Practically speaking, this means you don't have to suffer through two or three holes while the wheels continue to come off before making adjustments.

By using a solid post-shot routine, you can 1) learn more from each shot; 2) take corrective or adaptive actions sooner; and 3) identify trends and issues you may want to address later on the range.

On the range you'll benefit from the post-shot routine by enhancing your awareness and by activating your error detection and error correction capabilities. Every shot becomes a learning opportunity and a chance to refine the swing. When every ball counts, you'll really accelerate your learning and improvement!

I've written extensively about this process in ***The Practice Effect:***

How To Groove A Reliable, Automatic Golf Swing You Can Trust. When you are ready to take your game to the next level this book will be an invaluable companion on your journey.

Before you hit the ball, you use your pre-shot routine to rehearse the swing you intend to make. After you hit your shot you use a post-shot routine to evoke the memory and feel of the recent shot to understand how it was different from the rehearsal swings you made in the pre-shot routine. Comparing the intention of your shot to the reality of the results is the essence of the error-detection process, and it is where learning begins.

How To Implement A Post-Shot Routine

Once you've hit a shot you have a few precious seconds when the kinesthetic feel is still fresh in your awareness and your mental process is open to analysis. You'll want to take advantage of those seconds to learn from your shot.

You can implement your post-shot routine by asking yourself a number of questions similar to the ones below. With a little bit of practice you can mentally zip through these questions while the ball is still in flight. In other words, you can arrive at a complete analysis in just one to four seconds.

Odds are you already engage in some form of post-shot analysis (even if it is to say "S#$!"). Formalizing the process by using more "productive" feedback will help you get better faster.

Post-Shot Routine Starter Kit

Here are a series of questions that may serve as a starter kit for your post-shot routine.

- What just happened? (feedback from the direction, shape, and results of the shot: reality vs. intention).
- Why did it happen? (usually the underlying physics or mechanical causes of the issue. For example, a sliced drive usually results from an open clubface at impact).

- What caused it? (what were the mechanics that led to the result?).
- What changed (from my pre-shot rehearsal) and in what part of the swing did the change occur?
- What is the underlying root cause of the change? (was it a mental issue, alignment, or mechanical issue?).
- What was I supposed to do? (rehearse the correct motion and/ or thought process to see if it feels different than what just happened).
- What should my action or swing thought focus be for next swing? (focus on the next shot with correct intention).

Applying the Post Shot Routine

Think of the post-shot routine as akin to peeling away layers of an onion. The result of your shot will either match the mental image you rehearsed or it won't. If it matched, you reinforce the process. If it didn't, you start peeling the onion. In other words, you keep working backward from the results of the shot to identify the deepest, most fundamental root cause of the variance.

The first layer of the swing onion is observing the results vs. the intention. It's the "What." On the surface the answer is objective and visible. It will be some combination of direction, distance, and shape.

The second layer is what was going on at impact—what we call the "moment of truth." You can deduce that since the results were "X", then impact must have been "Y." In the example of a sliced drive, neither the direction nor the shape matched the intent, so at impact the slice (X) must have been caused by an open clubface (Y).

The next layer might be the underlying mechanics leading up to impact. In other words, you intuit that in order for "Y" to occur at impact, "Z" must have been going on during the swing. (This "Z" cause will be unique for every golfer, so for the sake of clarity I'll use the example of excess grip pressure for Z). You deduct that in order for your clubface to be open at impact (Y) you tightened your grip, just as you were starting your downswing (Z).

The next level deeper would be analyzing the underlying mental process just before or during the swing. You ask yourself the question "Why did I feel the need to use a death grip?" And with a little more digging you finally get to the root cause, discovering that somewhere during the swing you felt like you had to give it a little extra to get more distance, so you squeezed harder with your hands and tensed up your arms.

We say that golf is a mental game. Quite often the real underlying cause of a mechanical issue has its roots in some aspect of fear, uncertainty, or doubt (the FUD factor). To play your best golf you want to use your pre-shot routine to keep peeling back the onion until you get to the root cause. Then you address the real issue.

Once you have peeled the onion to arrive at the root cause you use the last step of the post-shot routine to rehearse (as you did in the pre-shot routine) what you should have done during the swing, so that by the time you get to your next shot the correct motion (and thought) is more likely to occur than the variance.

This entire process (except the corrective rehearsal swings) happens in a matter of seconds, so you can be confident that using a post-shot routine won't slow down your play. The results will be well worth the time you invest in developing a solid post-shot routine.

Here's an example of the internal conversation I had with myself during a recent round. Next to each thought I've put the "step" of the post-shot routine to provide context for how the process works. The whole dialogue occurred in mere seconds.

> "Wow. I just hit a big slice (what). Must have had an open clubface at impact (moment of truth). It felt like I was holding on with a death grip on the downswing (mechanical cause). Probably because I wanted to get a little extra distance and didn't entirely trust that I could do it (root mental cause). That's what made me tighten up. Darn. I didn't really need to get the extra distance. I just needed to put a good swing on it. What should I have done during that swing? I'll rehearse a

swing with a focus on maintaining consistent grip pressure and letting my club do the work (corrective rehearsal). Yep. I can feel the difference between my rehearsal swing and the swing that just happened. On my next shot I'm going to focus on being patient and on staying within my limits to put a good swing on it (positive intent for the next shot)."

14

TAKING IT TO THE COURSE

The Importance Of Single Swing Thoughts

You've just invested a substantial amount of time and energy reading and studying this book, and hopefully in practicing the drills and B.L.A.S.T. concepts. At some point you need to see it in action on the course.

The question is when. Here are my recommendations.

First, incorporate athletic balance into your play on the course *as fast as you can*. You may be able to incorporate athletic balance into your game after just one or two practice sessions.

Here is your strategy for bringing other elements of the distance keys and of the practice drills to the course: Practice them first on the range. Keep the B.L.A.S.T. Keys and drills (and the mechanical swing thoughts associated with them) on the range until you are ready.

How will you know when you are ready to use the B.L.A.S.T. concepts on the course?

- When you can reliably do a drill every time on each ball of your 5-ball set, and
- When the shot quality you produce from the drill or technique consistently produces a result you would rate as an 8, 9, or 10 in terms of shot quality, and
- When you can perform the drill or technique without conscious thought, or
- When using the drill or technique gives you more confidence than you would have had with your prior swing.

These Distance Keys and drills contain a tremendous amount of information. The last thing you need when you are playing, however, is a mind full of swing thoughts. It is the kiss of death to have multiple thoughts during a swing, especially when you are playing for a score.

Recall the three stages of learning outlined earlier. Swing thoughts originate in our neocortex, which means that with multiple swing thoughts on the golf course you would be swinging as though you were in the Cognitive Stage of learning. The Cognitive stage is characterized by jerky movements, which kills golf shots.

Rather, learn to play on automatic. Keep your thoughts simple. Practice the distance keys and drills enough so that you don't have to think about them. Work them into your pre-shot routine until they become automatic. That is the time to take them to the course. With correct, mindful practice, these distance keys will help you develop a tremendous amount of confidence, and, ultimately, a tremendous amount of swing speed which, as you now know, translates to distance.

There is much more information on the topic of effective practice, swing refinements, and playing better golf in my book ***The Practice Effect:*** *How To Groove A Reliable, Automatic Golf Swing You Can Trust.*

What You Should Do Next
Hit the range!

I hope you are fired up to start hitting longer drives. Because you have purchased this book I'll be sending a series of emails that will provide you with a plan to groove the concepts you've just read to help you begin to refine your swing. I recommend that you print those emails and put them in a binder. They'll give you a step-by-step, week-by-week, roadmap for implementing what you've read about in this book.

Think of the emails as a 5 Keys to Distance Companion that will help you APPLY the information in this book to YOUR OWN SWING in a manner that is cogent, realistic, and practical.

Your First Practice Plan

For now, your first week of your practice should focus on balance. Start with the balance drills in the first section. Review the videos before you head to the range. In your first week teach yourself what it means to swing in good balance.

Here's how you should plan your first few practices.

Grab a large bucket of balls. That should give you about 70 golf balls for your practice session.

First, warm up using the Baseball Rip swing. Pay attention to what the drill tells you about your balance—how well do you stay in balance? What is causing you to lose balance, and in what part of the swing? What adjustments can you make to stay in better balance?

Next, divide your bucket into 5-ball groups. During all these drills, focus on the FEEDBACK, not the results. Your goal is to develop your awareness, not hit great golf shots. The great golf shots will come!

Hit your first 5-ball set using the Tight Ankles drill. Pay attention to the feedback you get from the drill and make adjustments so you can learn to stay in better balance and swing without any wobble.

Move on to your second 5-ball set using the Happy Toes drill. As you set up and hit each ball, ask yourself "What adjustments am I making?" "How does my balance feel during the swing?"

Move on to your third 5-ball set and the Toe Tap drill. Learn what the drill will tell you about your ability to finish in balance. Ask yourself what adjustments you can make to finish perfectly balanced.

Now, cycle back through the drills. Try the Baseball Rip swing again and see if it feels different. Hit another 5-ball set using the Tight Ankles drill and see what feedback you get. Hit a 5-ball set using Happy Toes and pay attention to adjustments. Finish with a 5-ball set of Toe Taps and see if anything has changed or if your awareness has been activated.

You've just hit 30 balls! You're half-way through your practice and you are probably much more aware of your balance than you've ever been.

Now would be a good time to change gears and hit a 5-ball set of "normal" drives at a target or fairway. Use your full pre-shot and post-shot routines and simply focus on making balanced swings. Ask yourself how your awareness has changed.

Pay attention to the adjustments you make that help your swing feel more fluid and comfortable. Are they the same adjustments you made during the drills? You'll want to reinforce those adjustments. Can you start to hone in on areas of the swing where you tend to get out of balance? You'll focus some awareness in those areas in your next set of drills.

Next, start over at the beginning. Cycle through the Baseball Rip and the three balance drills once more in 5-ball sets. Finish with a fourth 5-ball set of "normal" drives to see if you are starting to incorporate athletic balance naturally into your swing.

You've just hit 60 balls! This is focused, intense practice. You'll be learning at a rapid clip. With this type of deep practice it won't take you more than a week or two to master the drills.

Use the last 10 balls in your bucket to play "simulated" golf holes. Imagine yourself on a hole (or holes) you know well and visualize how you would tee off on those holes. How will you use your new awareness to help you make better golf shots?

You can use this approach of practicing your three drills in rotation using 5-ball sets with each of the 5 B.L.A.S.T. Keys. I'll be sending you emails regularly to help you succeed. If you stick with it I'm confident that before long you'll be blasting 'em down the middle the way you've always wanted.

Thank you for your allowing me to share some golf wisdom with you. I appreciate your interest and wish you only the best in your endeavor to take it deep. I sincerely hope you will find the answers you need in this book. Don't forget to share your stories with me.

See you down the fairway!

Eric Jones, M.A. (Sport Psychology)
World Long Drive Champion
PGA Professional
Founder, Seaver Golf Academy
Founder, Target Centered Golf

INDEX

3-ball process 38
3-ball sets 39
5-ball groups 139
5-ball set 138-41

A

angle of approach ix-x, xii, 4, 8-10, 85, 122
arc width x, 71, 116
athletic balance 22, 27-8, 79, 88, 137, 140
athletic posture 22-3, 26-7
automatic stage of learning 17
awareness 15-16, 43, 61, 68, 73, 109-10, 131-3, 139-41
axis, tension-free 58-9, 108-9

B

backswing 27, 34, 38, 42-3, 45-6, 54-5, 57, 59-70, 72, 74-82, 86-8, 90-1, 93, 95-7, 106, 123-6
balance & posture 130-1
balance, dynamic 60
balance drills 31, 40, 48, 60, 118-19, 139-40
balance position 51
balanced position 27, 98
ball flight 11, 28
ball flight laws 13
baseball rip swing 40-1, 45-7, 90, 118, 139-40
baseball rip swing balance drill 31
baseball stride 92-3, 95
baseball stride drill 92-4
baseball stride hip speed drill 89
BLAST, summary 115
BLAST concepts, how to learn 117-18
BLAST keys, summary 115
bucket drills 67

C

center contact ix, xii, 7-8, 10
chicken wing 49-50
chicken wing position 104

closed club 13
club path 4, 11-12
clubface 8, 11, 65, 111, 134
    open 133-5
clubface angle 4, 110
clubface square 37
clubhead angle 7
cognitive stage of learning 17, 138
confidence 16, 110, 113, 138
consistency xii, 16, 53-4, 65, 76, 79, 88, 109, 124
core body rotation 37, 60

D

distance, effortless 18
district championships 4
drills
    arc width 73
    balance 31
    happy toes 27
    leverage 59
    low and slow 74, 77
    parallel clubs 81-3, 116
    patience 77
    pigeon -toe 66
    rhythm swinging 76
    slant board 61, 63
    sole plant 89-90
    speed of hips 89
    target extension 102
    tee forward extension 102
    tension-free swing 107
    tight ankles 31

E

extension 49-51, 72, 74-5, 80-3, 101, 103-5, 123
extension drills 102, 105, 107

F

feedback system 15-16, 28, 30, 39
finish position 32, 36, 38, 48, 51, 105-6
five-ball sets 119
    forward tee 103-4

G

golf stance   40-1, 50
grab   23-4, 70, 139
grip   9, 61-3, 109-11, 134
grip pressure   44, 59, 72-3, 91, 93-4, 96, 99, 110
grip pressure change   72, 110-11

H

habit   20, 46, 51, 104
heel plant drill   95-8
high finish   105-7
high finish extension drill   102
hip rotation   45, 47, 49-50, 86, 90, 96-8, 101
hip speed drill   89, 92, 95
hip turn   34, 40, 42, 45, 64, 85, 93-4, 98, 124-5
hook   11

I

impact zone   ix, 45, 49-50, 86, 91, 103, 106
integrative stage of learning   17

K

keys to distance   ix, xvi-xvii, 1, 18, 115

L

lag   21, 45-7, 72-3, 75, 85, 91, 111, 123
lag position   45, 101
launch angle   xv, 4, 9-10, 122
launch ballistics   xv-xvi
learning
  motor   117
  stages of   17-18, 138
Leith Anderson clubfitter   xvi
leverage   xii, 53-4, 57, 59, 64, 68, 70, 79-80, 85, 113, 116, 119
leverage drills   59-60, 64-5, 69-70
leverage position   54, 56-7, 60-3, 65-6, 69-71, 77, 80-1, 88, 90-1, 111, 124
leveraged top-of-backswing position   63
long drive   xvii, 3, 5, 9, 124
long drive championships   119, 124
long drive competitions   9, 73, 78
low and slow drill   74, 77

M

mental attitude, positive   18
mental picture   91, 106, 129-30
muscles

antagonistic   58-9, 107
  protagonistic   58, 107
myelin   19
myelination   19-20

N

neurons, myelinated   19-20

P

parallel clubs   81-3, 116
pathways, neural   18-19
physics, laws of   7, 13, 71
physiological constraints   49-50, 104
pigeon-toe drill   66
pivot   54, 61-3, 72, 87, 91, 95-6, 124
plane   74, 78, 81-2, 123
Player, Gary   94
post-shot routine   51, 127-8, 131-5, 140
  solid   132, 135
posture   23, 25-8, 33-4, 67, 90, 130
  balanced   27-8
power   27, 54-7, 59-60, 65, 67-8, 76, 86, 88, 96, 102, 110-11, 126
  dynamic   59, 107
  effortless   57, 60, 110
power axis   58
  tension-free   108
power loss   27, 37-8, 123
practice   117
Practice Effect   16, 112, 119, 132, 138
practice sessions   76, 115, 118-19, 137, 139
pre-shot routine   27, 104, 127-9, 131, 133, 135, 138
  sample   131
pre-shot routine keyword summary   131
pre-shot routine starter kit   130
pre-shot routine step-by-step   129
pressure   43, 66, 69-70, 92

R

random block practice   117-18
rehearsal swings   130, 133, 136
rehearse   133-5
release
  ball, club, hands, lag   9, 25, 46, 70, 72, 86, 94, 101, 109, 122-3
  early   72
  late   46-7
rhythm   33, 39, 41, 77, 128
rhythm swinging drill   76
rhythmic swings   44
right knee set leverage drill   59

S

self-awareness   15-16, 28, 30, 35, 39, 109
set-up position   25
shoulder turn   37, 123
signal strength, electrical   19
slant board   60-4, 80, 116
slant board drill   61, 63
slice   11-12, 56, 134-5
slide   54, 56, 61, 65-7
sliding   68, 80
sole plant drill   89-90
solid left side   29, 31, 34-5, 38
speed drills   89
spine, straight   27
spine angle   27, 65, 75
sport psychology   xvii, 141, 148
square contact   82-3
stacking   55, 57
straight left arm   37, 45-6, 72
swing arc   71, 73, 77-8, 81-3, 92, 119, 123
   wider   71-4, 79
swing arc drill   73-4, 78, 81
swing path   11-12, 82, 110
swing plane   21, 81-3
swing thought   29, 60, 105, 129, 138
swing tips   xi

T

takeaway   72, 74-5, 82, 108, 110, 123
   one-body   75

Target Centered Golf   ix, 141

target extension   98, 101-2, 105-6, 113, 116, 119
tee forward   102-5
tee forward extension drill   102
tension free   107-9, 113
tension free drill   108-9
tension free swing   43, 59, 92
tension free swing drill   107
tight ankles   29, 31, 35, 37-9, 118, 139-40
tight ankles balance drill   31
timing   47, 54, 56, 65, 72, 74-7, 92, 94
toe tap drill   48-9, 51
trust   16, 112, 119, 131, 133, 135, 138

W

waltz rhythm drill   77
weight shift   29, 31, 33, 35-8, 45, 48-9, 61-2, 68, 72, 80, 91-6, 98, 126
weight transfer   34, 93
world championships   3, 55

X

x-factor   58, 86, 123-4
x-factor power   86

Z

zone
   being in the   17
   impact   ix, 45, 49-50, 86, 91, 103, 106